DEMCO

from Animal Crackers to Wild West Beans

Easy and Fun Vegetarian Recipes for Healthy Babies and Children

Carol Timperley

Illustrations by Stephen May

CB
CONTEMPORARY BOOKS

Library of Congress Cataloging-in-Publication Data
is available from the United States Library of Congress

Cover design by Monica Baziuk
Cover and interior illustrations by Stephen May
Edited, designed, and produced by Eddison Sadd Editions Limited

First published in the United Kingdom in 1997 by Ebury Press, Random House,
20 Vauxhall Bridge Road, London SW1V 2SA
This edition is published by arrangement with Eddison Sadd Editions Limited
First published in the United States in 1998 by Contemporary Books
An imprint of NTC/Contemporary Publishing Company
4255 West Touhy Avenue, Lincolnwood (Chicago), Illinois 60646-1975 U.S.A.
Text copyright © 1997 by Carol Timperley
Illustrations © copyright 1997 by Stephen May
This edition © copyright 1997 by Eddison Sadd Editions

CONTENTS

INTRODUCTION

When my son was born, I was visited in the hospital by a resolutely childless and cynical chum. She cast a dismissive glance at the bundle that I, like all new mothers, firmly believed to be the most perfect human being ever created, helped herself to a glass of champagne and commented, "You do realize that it's all guilt and worry from here on?" Naturally, in my euphoria, I dismissed her comment as sour grapes. Four years later the resonance of those words is all too apparent. The desire to do the very best for our children, combined with a barrage of well-meaning advice, can conspire to make even the most competent parents feel inadequate at times. This is particularly true of diet. My aim in writing this book, however, is to give parents a practical and reassuring guide to vegetarian food, to help dispel the uncertainties that often surround vegetarian eating, and to give parents confidence that they are providing the best possible diet for their children.

While it has long been recognized that we are what we eat, expert opinion now suggests the degenerative diseases which plague our middle years are the direct result of a poor diet in childhood. Indeed, research has revealed children as young as eleven years old with partially clogged arteries and raised cholesterol levels; small time bombs waiting to explode into disaster zones of ill-health. In the light of this knowledge, it makes sense to give your child the best possible nutritional start in life.

It is my firm belief that the best possible nutritional start for a child means a vegetarian diet. As a parent, whether your reason for following a meat-free diet is ethical, environmental, or a matter of pure preference, from the point of view of your child's health the statistics speak for themselves. Research has proven that vegetarians suffer 30 percent less heart disease and 40 percent fewer cancers than meat eaters, and are 20 percent less prone to premature mortality. Vegetarians also enjoy lower incidences of all manner of diet-related disorders, from hypertension to hemorrhoids, food-poisoning to unsightly, health-threatening excess body fat.

Yet, while adults are increasingly turning toward a vegetarian diet, with the approval of health professionals, there is relatively little practical advice or support available for parents who wish to bring up their children as vegetarians. In fact, one of the medical textbooks I consulted while researching this book lists vegetarianism along with zen macrobiotic diets under "Dietary Abnormalities"! Such prejudice is not uncommon among the medical profession. My son's father is a cardiac surgeon and I have known more than one of his highly qualified colleagues to be more fazed at the prospect of a vegetarian dinner guest than a multiple coronary artery bypass. The situation is not helped by the "evangelical vegetarians" whose purist doctrine necessitates special shopping trips and hours of soaking legumes. I hope the advice offered in this book falls somewhere between the two extremes. (It is aimed at lacto-vegetarians, who consume milk and milk products, with or without eggs. Vegan parents should seek additional advice from their pediatrician.)

There is a common myth (perpetrated by those who perceive a vegetarian diet as a lifetime sentence to a steak-shaped gap on the dinner plate) that meat-free meals are time-consuming and complicated to make, and nutritionally inadequate. As all vegetarians know, this idea could not be more misguided. What could be quicker and simpler than a nutritious meal of beans on toast, or even a cheese sandwich? Furthermore, I think vegetarian babies tend to be bigger, brighter, and more resilient than their meat-eating peers.

As a busy working mother I understand all too well the pressures and constraints associated with juggling a career and family life. This is why you won't find in the following chapters any recipes which require soaking dried beans or other lengthy preparation processes. Nor am I opposed to the occasional jar of puréed vegetables or piece of chocolate—it's the close-up details, not the immediate outlook, that counts when feeding children. This said, when pressed for time, I would far rather my son ate a banana, a yogurt, and toast with beans than any of the so-called kids' menus available at a supermarket or carry-out near where we live.

If you opt to bring up your child as a vegetarian for ethical rather than health reasons, you may encounter the attitude that you are selfishly inflicting your own ideals on your child (as though food is the only area in which we make choices on our children's behalf!). In fact, most children instinctively veer toward a vegetarian diet. After all, meat is a fibrous, lumpy substance which requires effort to chew. Children have to work quite hard to acquire a taste for meat. I well recall one occasion when my son was invited for tea at a small friend's house and was served a pasta sauce containing chicken (I had failed to specify he did not eat meat). When I arrived to pick him I was told that he had diligently removed every chunk of chicken from the sauce.

The menu charts included in each chapter are no more than suggestions as to how you can combine recipes and basic foods to provide your child with a balanced diet. If you offer a wide variety of fresh foods, both cooked and raw, and observe the general principles of keeping sugar and salt to a minimum, you cannot go far wrong. Above all, bear in mind that, while food is primarily sustenance, a healthy diet of carefully, if simply, prepared fresh foods is a unique expression of our connection with our families, friends, and environment. An appreciation of good food is one of the greatest gifts you can give your child.

CHAPTER ONE

From Milk to Solids

Babies, it seems to me, are living proof of the theories of both chaos and perpetual motion. This is as true of your baby's eating patterns as it is of every other aspect of their development. No sooner have you come to grips with the whole milk business (when, how much, the best way to burp your baby), than they decide it's time to move onto the next stage. Just as you are certain that mashed banana never fails to please, they obstinately refuse anything and everything containing the faintest trace of it. It's almost as though they have an infallible instinct for detecting the split second that you feel really confident and they decide at that point to upset the apple-purée cart before you become complacent. And the more uptight Mom and Dad get, the better baby enjoys the game. When it comes to feeding children, if there is one golden rule it must be to remain relaxed.

For at least the first six months of life, the major source of nourishment is milk, which contains all the protein, vitamins, minerals, and fat required for healthy growth. Experts agree that breast milk is best for a variety of reasons—not least because it adapts to your growing baby's needs while also containing valuable antibodies and antibacterial agents to help increase resistance to disease. And, should you need convincing of the important role diet plays in development right from the start, recent studies to emerge from America suggest that children who were breast-fed as babies, even for just a few weeks, perform better academically at school than their bottle-fed peers.

From your point of view, breast feeding has the added advantages of costing nothing, and instantly providing milk at the correct temperature. If you breast feed your baby, it is important to pay close attention to your own diet and ensure that you eat plenty of vitamin- and calcium-rich foods (see the lists of foods on the following pages) and also drink plenty of water.

Even if you do breast feed, at some point during the first year of your baby's life you will probably want to substitute bottles for at least some of the milk feedings. (Not all breast-fed babies will accept a bottle. Some just refuse and get distraught and hungry, no matter who gives the bottle or how early. Others readily accept a bottle, and some even prefer a bottle to the breast.) If you do decide to substitute a bottle, you should always choose a commercial formula and never use cow's milk. Always read the label carefully (some formulas contain non-dairy animal fats—your pediatrician should be able to advise) and follow the instructions for making up the formula to the letter, because the wrong concentration of powder to fluid can be harmful. Use sterile or boiled water that has been allowed to cool (boil water for 5 minutes).

Once your child is twelve months old you may safely introduce whole cow's milk as a drink. Cow's milk is suitable for cooking purposes from about six months, as are other dairy products such as cheese and yogurt. (However, there are benefits in continuing to use formula or breast milk even in cooking after six months as it does provide additional nutrients.)

Bottles, nipples, and other utensils you use to prepare formula or in feeding your baby must be cleaned thoroughly because of the risk of bacteria. If the water in your home is chlorinated, you can simply use your dishwasher or wash the utensils in hot tap water with dishwashing detergent and then rinse them in hot tap water. If you have well water or nonchlorinated water, place the utensils in boiling water for 5–10 minutes. It is wise to ensure that at least 2½ cups of milk a day is taken for the first two years. For vegetarian children especially, it is a valuable source of protein and vitamin B_{12}.

A Matter of Substance

For a host of reasons (see page 19), it is not a good idea to attempt to wean your baby from milk to a diet of solid food too early, and certainly never before the age of four months. However, by about six months you should be introducing solids because it is thought that the supplies of iron with which your baby is born begin to run out at about this time. Of course, the foods you offer your baby at this initial stage of weaning will be anything but solid, but they represent a marked contrast to milk, in texture and taste. Simple non-wheat cereal (baby rice), fruit, and vegetable purées are the ideal supplements to milk. There is no need to concern yourself too much in these early stages with nutritional or caloric values—the idea is really to get your baby used to the business of eating. However, as you progress to the next stage of weaning, when solids form a more significant part of your baby's diet, it becomes important to think about food values.

Balancing Act

The phrase "a balanced diet" seems designed to strike trepidation in the heart of anyone lacking a dietitian's qualifications or a degree in foodscience, implying as it does the need for scales, calculators, and mathematical equations. In fact, there is no great mystique about a balanced diet. This simply means eating a variety of foods chosen from each of the six major nutrient groups: proteins, carbohydrates, fats, vitamins, minerals, and water.

As long as you include at least some of these in your baby's diet each day, the remarkably clever computer that is the body will do the rest. The six major nutrient groups that you need concern yourself with are as follows.

PROTEINS

Protein is essential for the growth and repair of body tissue. Many misconceptions surround the ability of a vegetarian diet to supply adequate amounts of protein for a growing child. The confusion arises because proteins are made up of some 20 amino acids, roughly half of which the body can make itself and the remainder of which (known as essential amino acids) need to be supplied by food. While animal proteins contain all of the essential amino acids, individual plant proteins may contain lower amounts of some of them and therefore need to be eaten in combination.

For vegetarians who eat dairy products this is not a problem, and even those who do not eat dairy foods receive more than adequate supplies of amino acids simply by eating a variety of protein foods. In fact, be reassured that it is almost impossible not to eat sufficient protein (assuming sufficient food is eaten), and most Western diets contain more protein than is needed, which can place a strain on the kidneys. Good vegetarian sources of protein include milk and milk products, such as cheese and yogurt; eggs; soy products, such as tofu and textured vegetable protein (TVP); all nuts (see page 14) and seeds; beans and peas, such as lentils and kidney beans; and grains, such as wheat, barley, and rice.

There was a time when people thought it necessary to balance vegetable proteins so the proper amount of each amino acid would be present at each meal. This view of "food combining" is nutritionally out of date, as it is now known that the body has a short-term store of essential amino acids and therefore a balance of amino acids can be taken over the course of a day rather than at each meal. Vegetarians eating a mixture of grains, legumes, seeds, nuts, and vegetables will be consuming a balance of amino acids without any planning. For vegetarian babies and children, breast milk, formula, or cow's milk, eggs; and milk products such as cheese, yogurt and milk-based desserts (not cream or butter), provide complete protein. Meals such as beans on toast, nut butter or cheese sandwiches, cereal with milk, or rice with peas, beans, or lentils are good examples of simple meals which contain a reasonable balance of amino acids.

CARBOHYDRATES

Carbohydrates are vital for growth and providing energy, and the starchy variety should be the most abundant nutrient in the diets of adults and young children.

However, while a high-fiber diet (containing plenty of foods such as whole-wheat bread and pasta) is desirable for adults, you do not want to focus on a high-fiber diet for infants. While avoiding refined sugars (found in candy, cookies, cakes, and commercial sweetened drinks) wherever possible, do bear in mind that high-fiber diets can conflict with the intense nutritional requirements of growing infants, filling them up before they have obtained sufficient nutrients for healthy growth and development. Provided your child eats plenty of fruit, there is absolutely nothing wrong in allowing meals to include white bread and pasta rather than the whole-wheat versions (there are even certain advantages). Good sources of carbohydrate include all fruits and vegetables; breakfast cereals, bread, and pasta; starchy vegetables, such as potatoes and peas; and legumes.

As children get older, more whole-grain foods, such as whole-wheat bread and pasta, brown rice, and whole-grain cereals, should be eaten to avoid constipation, promote healthy eating habits, and also provide a useful source of B vitamins. It is best to avoid any products with added bran, such as bran-flake cereals, which can cause digestive problems and prevent the absorption of some minerals.

FATS

Despite having become almost as taboo as the other F-word in recent times, fats provide a concentrated source of energy and, in young children, are important for the healthy development of the brain and nervous system. In fact it is saturated fats, implicated in many of the degenerative diseases to which the Western world is prone, which give this necessary food group its bad reputation.

For vegetarians, the good news is that saturated fat comes almost exclusively from animal products, so, provided you regulate the amount of dairy products in your child's diet and use good-quality vegetable oils such as olive oil for cooking, you will be making a great contribution to safeguarding his or her future health. However, it is vital you do not attempt to feed your child low-fat dairy products for at least the first two years because milk fat is a valuable source of energy and fat-soluble vitamins. Other good sources of fat are vegetable oils such as soybean, sunflower, corn, and olive oil; margarine (nonhydrogenated varieties are best); avocados; and nuts.

Hydrogenated fats should be avoided for babies, children, and pregnant and breast-feeding women because they contain trans fatty acids, which can interfere with the essential fatty acids vital to healthy brain development. This is particularly important for vegetarians since their bodies make these nutrients rather than obtaining them from fish oil. Hydrogenated fats are found in some margarines and many commercial food products, so you need to read the manufacturers' labels.

VITAMINS

Vitamins are essential for correct body functioning, and certain antioxidant vitamins (A, C, and E) are now thought to play a major role in protecting against cancer. There are two main types of vitamins: fat soluble and water soluble. The fat-soluble vitamins (A, D, E, and K) can be stored by the body, but the water-soluble vitamins (C and B complex, except B_{12}) cannot, so they need to be supplied on a daily basis. Because, as their name implies, they dissolve in water, this latter group of vitamins can also be destroyed by overzealous cooking. So, fruit and vegetables should be lightly cooked, preferably steamed, or served raw wherever possible. Vitamin K is made by bacteria in the gut, but, as new-born babies do not have these bacteria,

VITAMINS IN FOCUS

VITAMIN A
Necessary for growth, healthy skin and tooth enamel, and good vision. Good sources:

Carrots • Spinach • Green Leafy Vegetables • Watercress • Peppers • Dried Apricots

VITAMIN B GROUP
Necessary for growth, for the conversion of food into energy, a healthy nervous system, and for the formation of red blood cells. Good sources:

Green Leafy Vegetables • Wheat Germ • Whole Grains • Beansprouts • Bananas • Avocados • Mushrooms • Peanuts • TVP • Fortified Breakfast Cereals • Margarine • Dairy Products

VITAMIN C
Necessary for growth, healthy body tissue, wound healing, and resistance to infection. Also aids in iron absorption so it is especially important for vegetarians, because plant-derived iron deposits are less readily absorbed than those found in meat. Good sources:

Green Leafy Vegetables • Broccoli • Cabbage • Peppers • Parsley • Potatoes • Peas • Citrus and Berry Fruits

VITAMIN D
Necessary for the formation of healthy bones and teeth. Can be manufactured by the body when the skin is exposed to sunlight, but it is also found in:

Dairy Products • Fortified Cereals • Margarine

VITAMIN E
Necessary for the maintenance of the body's cell structure. Good sources:

Vegetable Oils • Wheat Germ • Nuts • Seeds • Avocados

VITAMIN K
Necessary for blood-clotting. Good sources:

Green Leafy Vegetables • Vegetable Oils • Whole Grains

they are routinely given an injection of vitamin K, usually before leaving the delivery room.

As fruit and vegetables are rich in vitamins, vegetarian children tend to have an adequate vitamin intake without the supplements often prescribed to children by pediatricians. Vitamin B_{12} and vitamin D, frequently cited as areas of concern for vegetarians, are present in adequate amounts in all dairy products, in fortified breakfast cereals, and, in the case of vitamin D, in most vegetable margarines.

MINERALS IN FOCUS

CALCIUM

Calcium is necessary for the formation of healthy bones and teeth and is therefore particularly important for growing children. Good sources of calcium:

Dairy Products • Tofu • Green Leafy Vegetables • Almonds • Brazil Nuts •Sesame Seeds

IRON

Iron is necessary for the formation of red blood cells. While it is present in many plant foods, the body does not absorb iron from plant sources as readily as from animal sources. A diet rich in whole foods compounds this problem. However, if vitamin C is taken at the same time as iron-rich foods, absorption is markedly increased. Good sources of iron:

Tofu • Beans • Legumes• Spinach • Cabbage • Wheat Germ • Whole Grains • Dried Fruits

ZINC

Zinc is vital to many body functions, including growth. Good sources of zinc:

Whole Grains • Beans and Peas • Pumpkin and Sesame Seeds • Dairy Products • Nuts

MINERALS

Like vitamins, minerals cannot be manufactured by the body and therefore need to be supplied by the diet. Although the body requires some fifteen different minerals, the three most important in relation to a vegetarian diet are iron, calcium, and zinc.

Drinking large amounts of cow's milk can interfere with the absorption of iron. If, between the ages of one and two years old, your child is drinking 24–32 ounces of milk or less a day there's little cause for concern. If your child drinks much more than that and won't be persuaded to eat more iron-rich foods, consult your pediatrician about adding an iron supplement.

WATER

Up until the age of about six months your baby normally obtains enough fluid from milk. In certain circumstances—such as in exceptionally hot weather or during a stomach upset—you may wish to offer additional fluid in the form of cooled boiled tap water. If, however, your baby is vomiting and has diarrhea and these symptoms persist for more than twenty-four hours, seek medical advice, since young babies can dehydrate very rapidly, with potentially serious consequences. Once your baby is taking solids, you should offer regular drinks in addition to the milk feedings as long as he or she continues to eat well (some babies have a tendency to fill themselves with fluids then refuse their food).

Although there are many commercially available herbal and fruit drinks specifically for babies, all of these are rich in sugar, which can harm developing teeth, so water remains the best choice. If you decide to give fruit juices (if, for example, your baby seems reluctant to take water), always dilute them as much as possible and give them in a training cup (never a bottle) to minimize the risk of damage to teeth. Carbonated drinks are unsuitable because they fill children with air, not nourishment.

Allergies and Additives

An allergy is an abnormal reaction to any food or substance. Most typically an allergy manifests itself in the form of rashes, stomach upsets, swelling, and hyperactive behavior. Thankfully, allergies are fairly rare, although some experts believe they are on the rise. Common food allergens include dairy products, wheat, citrus fruits, and nuts (see right). When there is a family history of allergy, these foods should be introduced with caution.

There is considerable evidence to suggest babies who are breast-fed are less susceptible to developing allergies, as are those who are weaned slightly later than average. These points may be worth considering if you suspect a hereditary allergy. Many widely used food additives, such as the food coloring tartrazine (Yellow No. 5), are associated with allergic reactions in children, so it makes sense to avoid these. More difficult to cope with are allergies to basic foods such as cow's milk, a particular problem for babies who are bottle-fed. Soy milk formulas are available, but should be given

to healthy full-term infants only when medically necessary. But some pediatricians prescribe soy milk from birth as a preventive measure when there is a strong family history of allergies to cow's milk.

Food intolerances are conditions where the body is incapable of digesting certain substances. Lactose and gluten intolerance are the most serious, but fortunately they are rare.

NUTS

Nuts should always be ground for under-fives because of the risk of choking. Whole nuts must be chewed with a grinding motion and children don't master this type of chewing until age four. Peanuts should still not be given to children until age seven or older. If peanut butter is given, avoid large spoonfuls because these can be difficult for young children to chew and swallow. Nut allergies are increasingly common in children and can be severe. Very recent research suggests there is room for concern, particularly in families with a history of allergies, eczema, or asthma. Some researchers suggest that children in such families should refrain from eating nuts until the age of three and that other families would do no harm in introducing them a little later than presently suggested by accepted guidelines.

Soy Milk and Soy Products

Soy milk formulas are recommended for babies in only exceptional circumstances because soy naturally contains high levels of phyto-estrogens, which can mimic natural hormones. This may have some benefits for adult women (in protecting against breast cancer), but could upset a baby's delicate hormone balance. At the time of writing, baby-milk manufacturers are looking to reduce the amounts of phyto-estrogens in soy milk formula. Vegan mothers, who avoid all dairy products, have a strong incentive to continue breast feeding for the first two years of life.

It is fine to introduce foods such as tofu (soy bean curd), soy milk, and soy burgers and sausages to a child over one as part of a varied vegetarian diet.

A Matter of Convenience

In an ideal world, every morsel that passed our children's lips would be lovingly and freshly prepared from the finest natural ingredients. However, few of us are fortunate enough to manage this. Inevitably, there will be occasions when it is necessary to resort to convenience foods. Try not to torture yourself with guilt when this happens; the occasional package or jar is not going to adversely affect your baby's growth and development (although relying on such foods exclusively may, if only in relation to his palate).

When buying convenience foods, read the label or package carefully and reject any foods with a high content of hydrogenated fat, sugar (maltodextrin, dextrose, sucrose), salt, or bulk-ing agents such as modified starch. It is now possible to buy organic baby foods in jars, and these are preferable to other types. For emer-gencies, many ordinary food products are suit-able for babies: for example, canned baked beans (choose one of the low-sugar, low-salt varieties); canned fruits in natural juice; and canned vegetables such as corn, peas, and beans in water, without added salt or sugar.

GETTING THE TIMING RIGHT

There are few hard and fast rules about the age at which it magically becomes safe to introduce certain foods. The important thing is to introduce new foods in the order suggested below. The list is intended as a guideline only. By the age of 12 months or so, your baby should be able to enjoy most foods, prepared appropriately (with the exception of whole nuts).

FIRST STAGE OF WEANING: 4–6 MONTHS
Apples • Apricots • Avocados • Bananas • Carrots • Cauliflower • Leeks • Mangoes • Melons • Peaches • Pears • Potatoes and Sweet Potatoes • Rice

SECOND STAGE OF WEANING: 6–9 MONTHS
Beets • Berry Fruits • Bread • Broccoli • Cabbage • Celery • Citrus Fruits • Cherries • Dairy Products (butter, cheese, cream, yogurt) • Eggplant • Grapes • Lentils (split), puréed • Mushrooms • Oats • Onions • Pasta • Peas • Peppers • Pineapple • Seeds • Sprouts • Tomatoes • Zucchini

THIRD STAGE OF WEANING: 9–12 MONTHS
Beans and Peas • Nuts, ground (optional) • Peanut Butter • Salads

12 MONTHS AND ABOVE
Seasoning • Yeast Extract • Cow's Milk (whole)

Some commercially produced cereals are also acceptable for babies and young children; Weetabix and Shredded Wheat in particular.

Frozen fruit and vegetables make acceptable alternatives to fresh vegetables, and they may be richer in nutrients. If you do use frozen vegetables, choose packages from the bottom of the freezer case (their temperature will be lower than those nearer the top), and pack them in an insulated bag to prevent defrosting on the journey home.

Hygiene

When preparing and cooking food for babies and young children, it is important to be scrupulous about your own and your kitchen hygiene. Always wash your hands thoroughly (preferably using one of the many excellent antibacterial hand soaps) before touching any food intended for your baby. Make sure that all surfaces are clean; ideally, they should be wiped daily using one of the many available antibacterial agents. If you have pets, never allow them anywhere near the areas where you prepare your baby's food.

Pay particular attention to the cleanliness of dishcloths, dish towels, and cutting boards, all of which can harbor germs. (Plastic or glass cutting boards are preferable to wood.) Utensils should be washed in hot, soapy water and rinsed well, so no traces of detergent remain. Avoid nonstick pans, since their surfaces have a tendency to "pit" and trap particles of food, thus creating a potential source of contamination. Aluminum pans should also be avoided since there is some question as to whether the aluminum metal is absorbed by food cooked in such pans. Make sure that your refrigerator is operating at the correct temperature—a thermometer designed for this purpose is a good investment.

During the first stage of weaning sterilize your baby's spoons and bowls along with the bottles. This is no longer necessary after six months, although bottles and nipples used for milk should be sterilized for as long as your baby continues to use them.

Food Preparation

Most vegetables and fruits, except those grown organically, are sprayed with pesticides. Since no one can offer any guarantees about the long-term safety of even minute traces of these chemicals, it makes sense to peel all fruit and vegetables. Always cook fruit and vegetables for the minimum possible time to preserve as many nutrients as possible (except pulses and legumes, which need boiling rapidly for at least 10 minutes to destroy toxins). Peas and beans should be cooked until tender so that they are easily digested. To avoid adding fat, choose steaming and microwaving methods.

Never add salt to your baby's food. Herbs may be used to vary the flavor of a dish and, at the second stage of weaning, a modest amount of spice. For toddlers, alcohol is a perfectly acceptable ingredient, since the alcohol evaporates during cooking, leaving only the flavor.

Frozen Assets

When preparing meals for your baby, you will almost inevitably find you have a surplus because portions are so small. It's worth freezing this surplus immediately so you have a stock of foods for those occasions when you have no time to cook. (It is not advisable to store food for babies in the refrigerator for any length of time. If food cannot be frozen, make just enough for immediate use.) Use the freezing symbol at the end of some recipes as a guide to which foods freeze best.

To begin with, ice-cube trays are ideal for freezing baby-size portions, but, as your baby's appetite increases, clean yogurt cartons or similar-size containers become more suitable (see pages 20–1). Don't stock up for months; your baby's appetite and preferences will change so rapidly during this period it would be imprudent to plan more than four weeks ahead. Also, while freezing is a good method of preserving food, the nutritional value of frozen food does diminish with time.

The Recipes

All the recipes included in the following chapters are ones which my son has tried and tested and, on occasion (remember, babies' tastes are fickle), enjoyed. The number of portions is given in every case, but these can only be approximate, because appetites vary enormously. I am confident that the recipes introduce children to a wide spectrum of flavors and cuisines, while guaranteeing they receive at the same time the widest possible range of nutrients to aid healthy growth and development. Adapt the recipes to suit your own family's taste, register the reaction in the box provided, and, above all, enjoy the unique experience of feeding your child.

CHAPTER TWO

First Flavors

FOUR TO SIX MONTHS

Somewhere between the ages of four and six months, most babies begin to show signs that they are ready for their first taste of real food. To begin with, the amount eaten will be quite literally just a taste, but it is still well worth the time and trouble to prepare homemade fruit and vegetable purées, as the flavors experienced in these early days will determine your baby's food preferences over the coming months and years.

As all new mothers quickly learn, myself included, parental peer-group pressure positively explodes once hitherto sensible individuals produce an offspring on which to foist their thwarted ambitions. The obvious extremes (flash cards at four weeks, analyses of Mozart operas at six months) are easy to dismiss, but when it comes to ordinary milestones like weaning and walking, such pressure can become insidious. I well remember the totally irrational sense of failure I experienced on returning home with my still contentedly breast-fed, twelve-week-old son from a routine doctor's visit where I had discovered that several babies of the same age had already started on solids. Did this mean my son's development was arrested? What if his growth were stunted?

At this stage, as at every other stage, all babies are individuals who develop at their own pace. Moreover, experts agree that there is no advantage whatsoever in early weaning, but there are several very real disadvantages. Until your baby is at least four months old, the digestive system is not mature enough to cope with anything other than milk, which contains all the necessary vital nutrients. By introducing solid foods too early you run the risk of reducing your baby's appetite for the milk he or she needs to grow and thrive, and increasing the chance of stomach upsets and food allergies. While some babies are obviously ready for solids at four months, others continue to gain weight and show no interest in foods other than milk until at least six months. Bottle-fed babies tend to start on solids earlier than breast-fed ones, probably because formula milk does not adapt to the baby's changing requirements as breast milk does.

Let your own baby guide you as to when he or she is ready for solids. Look for the tell-tale indications, such as putting toys and objects in the mouth, demanding feedings at shorter intervals and seeming less satisfied, and showing an interest in your meals (perhaps reaching out for your food).

How to Wean Your Baby

For a baby used to sucking, eating is a new skill that must be mastered. It takes time to get used to the idea. Begin by offering a little solid food just once a day—lunchtime is usually best because then your baby will be most alert. Avoid evening because, in the unlikely event that a new food disagrees with your baby, you could then both have a disturbed night.

Prepare no more than a tablespoon of tepid rice or a single fruit or vegetable purée (see Basic Purées, pages 23–9). Start by giving half the normal breast or bottle feeding (otherwise your baby will be too hungry to concentrate on the new experience and you'll both become frustrated), then dip the end of a baby spoon in the purée. Introduce the spoon between your baby's lips (don't push it in as this causes gagging) and allow him or her to lick the food off. The first spoonful may just be spat out, but don't force things, simply try again. After a few attempts, or when about a teaspoonful has been eaten (the reason for the discrepancy between amounts prepared and consumed will immediately become apparent!), clean your baby's mouth and resume milk feeding.

For the first two or three weeks, offer the same food for at least three days to enable your baby to become accustomed to it and you to monitor reactions. After about three weeks, increase the amount to about four teaspoons and introduce a little baby rice halfway through the breakfasttime feeding. Once your baby is happily taking this amount, start to introduce a little solid food at dinner, then offer two courses at lunch: a vegetable purée followed by a fruit purée. Within two to three months you should find your baby is eating solids three times a day and no longer requires a milk feeding at lunchtime (when your baby is thirsty, offer cooled, boiled water in a training cup).

Good First Foods

Most fruit and vegetables are suitable first foods for babies, although citrus and berry fruits are best avoided at first since they can be too acidic for immature digestive systems. Always wash, peel, and cook fruit and vegetables thoroughly (I have indicated in the recipes on the following pages the few instances where this is unnecessary), and purée the flesh to a very smooth consistency. Often you will find that extra liquid is required to make the consistency of the purée acceptable to your baby. This liquid can be boiled water or, preferably, breast or bottle milk. Do not replace breast or formula milk, even in cooking, until your baby is at least six months old. Note that there are nutritional advantages in continuing longer with such a milk, designed as it is specifically for human babies.

Proteins, such as cheese, yogurt, cream, eggs, and legumes, should also be avoided until weaning is firmly established. The gluten-free cereals (that is, rice, millet, and corn) may be introduced from the very beginning, but wait until your baby is happily tolerating these (and certainly not before six months) before attempting to introduce wheat and oats. Avoid baby oat cereal unless the flakes are very finely ground.

And, however bland these first foods may seem to your sophisticated adult palate, never be tempted to add salt or sugar to food intended for your baby; salt will harm the kidneys, and sugar will just educate your baby to expect sweet foods. The natural sweetness of fruit and some vegetables, particularly root vegetables, is adequate.

Equipment

You don't need a great deal of special equipment to prepare food for your baby, but certain items do make the process much simpler. A food processor or blender saves a lot of time and wrist work. Although I already had a food processor, I found a mini version invaluable, since small quantities seem to get lost and process unevenly in a larger bowl. Also, however scrupulous one is about cleaning such dishes, strong flavors such as garlic and chili do have a tendency to linger. A nylon strainer is essential for foods with seeds or tough fibers.

If you plan to make batches of baby food (anything over a tablespoon constitutes a batch at this stage), a couple of plastic ice-cube trays are ideal for freezing the surplus. Keep the trays exclusively for baby food and defrost one or two cubes as required.

If you haven't already, invest in an adequate supply of plastic-backed bibs to protect your child's clothes—you'll be amazed at just how far one teaspoonful of puréed carrot can spread. (I began weaning my son at about the same time that he learned to blow raspberries; as a result, our wallpaper featured an interesting multicolored, textured effect for some time.) If you plan to feed your baby sitting on your lap rather than in a bouncy chair or portable car seat, buy a capacious apron for yourself, too.

Most drugstores and baby-equipment stores sell reasonably priced, plastic weaning spoons, which have chunky square tips and so are easy for your baby to lick food from. A couple of small plastic bowls with handles and suction bases are also a good idea. You'll also need a training cup with a spout. Since this will spend a great deal more time horizontal than vertical, be sure the lid fits securely to avoid spilling the contents.

Hygiene

It is especially important to practice good kitchen hygiene when preparing food for young babies, because their delicate digestive systems and low resistance make them especially vulnerable to infections. Wipe kitchen surfaces with an antibacterial solution at least once a day and change hand towels, dish towels, and dishcloths daily. A dishwasher is the best method of cleaning cooking utensils, and your baby's cups, dishes, and spoons, but if you don't have one, wash dishes thoroughly in hot soapy water, rinse well, and allow to drain until dry. If it is necessary to dry dishes and utensils, use paper towels rather than dish towels, which can harbor germs.

Always discard any food which is left in your baby's dish (bacteria from the spoon may contaminate it) and warm defrosted food only once. Wash your hands religiously before preparing food for your baby, and try to get into the habit of washing his or her hands before, as well as after, mealtimes. Grubby little fists make great breeding grounds for all sorts of undesirable bacteria. Stomach upsets are distressing for your baby but even more so for you, so it is worth taking these precautions to prevent problems.

Baby Rice

Most health professionals recommend baby rice as the very first solid food for babies, because it is nutritious, easy to digest, and free from gluten. While there are many excellent commercial varieties available, it is easy—and much cheaper—to prepare your own. Many mothers are deterred from doing so by the enticing list of fortifying nutrients on the packages of commercial rice, but at this stage your baby still obtains all the necessary nutrients from milk, so added nutrients are an unnecessary luxury. Always use white rice since young babies cannot easily digest brown rice. Keep a supply of cooked rice in the freezer, since it can be added to any of the following purées, providing extra volume.

MAKES 12–16 PORTIONS

⅓ cup short-grain white rice

Wash the rice thoroughly under running water. Place in a small saucepan and add sufficient boiling water to cover by approximately ¼ inch. Stir once, cover with a tight-fitting lid, and simmer very gently for 30–40 minutes, until all the water is absorbed and the grains are very tender. Purée with breast or formula milk to a smooth, creamy consistency.

Basic Purées

Simple fruit and vegetable purées are the ideal first foods for your baby. As he or she becomes more accustomed to solids you can start to experiment with combinations of fruits and vegetables, but to begin with it is best to serve them individually. You will then be able to identify the flavors your baby enjoys, those that are likely to be an acquired taste, and those that actively disagree with him or her.

The quantities given for the single purées are the smallest that it is feasible to prepare. In the early stages of weaning they may be sufficient for three or four "meals," but you will soon find the whole amount disappears at one sitting. Then is the time to double or quadruple quantities and freeze the surplus for future use. Where extra liquid is specified, use breast or formula milk, preferably, or boiled water.

APPLE

I found Newtown Pippins were a particularly successful variety for purées.

1 *small apple*

Rinse, peel, core, and chop the apple. Place in a small saucepan with a little water. Bring to a boil, cover, and simmer until very tender, 5–8 minutes. Purée to a smooth consistency, adding extra liquid if necessary.

APRICOT

In the early stages of weaning, try combining apricot purée with baby rice. After banana, this was my son's favorite first food.

3 *fresh ripe apricots*

Rinse, peel, halve, and pit the fruits. Place in a small saucepan with a little water. Bring to a boil, cover, and simmer until tender, 10–15 minutes. Purée until smooth, adding extra liquid if necessary.

BANANA

Banana is one of the very few fruits that can safely be given uncooked to babies in the early stages of weaning. However, do be warned that the fruit fibers may at first pass through your baby undigested! Choose a very ripe, unblemished fruit.

½ *small banana*

Mash the banana with a fork until no lumps remain. Add sufficient breast or formula milk to give a smooth consistency.

PEAR

Once solid feeding has been established, there is no need to cook ripe pears before puréeing. In the initial stages, however, light cooking makes the fruit easier for your baby to digest.

1 *small ripe pear*

Rinse, peel, and core the pear. Place in a small saucepan with a little water. Bring to a boil, cover, and simmer until very soft, 5–8 minutes, depending on the variety of pear. Purée to a smooth consistency, adding extra liquid if necessary.

PEACH

Ripe peaches are a perfect first food for babies: sweet, succulent, and very juicy.

1 *small ripe peach*

Rinse the peach, then skin by scoring a cross in the skin and submerging the fruit in boiling water for 10–30 seconds. The skin should then lift away with ease. Peel, pit, and chop the fruit and place in a small saucepan with a little water. Bring to a boil, cover, and simmer until tender, about 10 minutes. Purée the cooked peach flesh to a smooth consistency, adding extra liquid if necessary.

PRUNE

Although many adults have an aversion to prunes (considered more remedy than food), babies seem to love them. You may find they do have a laxative effect, but I found this was largely counteracted by mixing them with an equal quantity of baby rice. Later on, try combining prunes with mashed banana.

5 *pitted prunes*

Rinse the prunes thoroughly and place in a small saucepan. Cover with cold water. Bring to a boil and simmer for 20–30 minutes or until very tender. Purée to a smooth consistency, adding extra liquid if necessary.

MANGO

Use the small, yellow Indian Alphonso mangoes (if you can find them) rather than the larger, green African ones which are more widely available. Although the Alphonso mangoes are only briefly in season, their milder, sweeter flavor is perfect for babies.

1 *small mango*

Scrub the mango thoroughly and peel. Cut the flesh away from the pit. Purée to a smooth consistency.

MELON

Any variety of melon can be fed to a baby, provided the melon is very ripe and the skin is well washed before you cut into it. However, I think that Galia melons tend to be sweeter than other varieties. If the fruit is not entirely ripe, steam it lightly before puréeing.

1 *small wedge melon*

Cut the melon flesh away from the skin, removing all of the slightly greener fruit close to the skin. Purée to a smooth consistency. Because melons contain a high proportion of water, it should not be necessary to add extra liquid.

ZUCCHINI

Zucchini is both bland in flavor and easy to digest, making it an ideal first food. Avoid very large specimens since, despite their prize-winning potential at local produce shows, these can prove dry and fibrous.

1 *thick slice zucchini*

Peel the zucchini and chop the flesh into cubes. Steam it over boiling water for 10–15 minutes or until tender. Mash the flesh with a fork until smooth.

CARROT

Carrots seems universally popular with young babies, probably because of their natural sweetness. Use young, tender specimens since these tend to be less fibrous.

1 *medium carrot*

Scrub the carrot thoroughly, cut off the tip and root, and peel. Place in a pan of lightly boiling water. Cover and simmer for about 30 minutes or until very tender. Drain, reserving the cooking liquid, and purée to a smooth consistency, adding as much of the reserved liquid as necessary.

AVOCADO

Avocados are highly nutritious, and their lovely creamy texture and bland taste are ideal for babies. They also have the advantage of being one of the few "instant" foods you can offer a young baby. Choose a soft, ripe fruit and prepare avocado immediately before your baby is ready to eat to prevent the flesh from discoloring.

1 *slice medium-ripe avocado*

Mash the flesh (using a fork) or purée, adding breast or formula milk to give the desired consistency.

POTATO

For young babies, "old" baking varieties of potato are best, since they fall apart when cooked and therefore mash better. Choose a specimen with as smooth and unblemished a skin as possible.

1 *medium potato*

Scrub the potato, peel, and cut out any blemishes. Cut the potato into evenly sized chunks. Place in a saucepan of boiling water. Cover and simmer until very tender, 20–30 minutes. Drain and mash (using a fork) to a smooth consistency, adding breast or formula milk if extra liquid is required.

PARSNIP

In common with other root vegetables, parsnip has a natural sweetness which immediately appeals to babies' palates. Choose small, young parsnips, which have the best flavor and texture.

1 *medium parsnip*

Scrub the parsnip, trim away the root and tip, and cut into quarters lengthwise. Cut away the woody core and chop the parsnip into evenly sized pieces. Place in a saucepan of boiling water. Cover and simmer for 25–30 minutes or until very tender. Purée to a smooth consistency, adding extra liquid if necessary.

SWEET POTATO

The creamy orange flesh of this cousin to the white potato appeals especially to babies. You can boil sweet potato as above, but I prefer to bake it.

1 *small sweet potato*

Scrub the potato skin, dry it, and prick all over with a fork. Bake at 400°F for ¾–1 hour or until soft. Split the skin, scoop out the flesh, and mash (using a fork) to a smooth consistency, adding breast or formula milk.

CAULIFLOWER

In the early stages of weaning, make sure that cauliflower is very well cooked, otherwise it can give your baby uncomfortable gas.

3–4 *cauliflower flowerets*

Wash the cauliflower well. Place it in a saucepan of boiling water. Cover and simmer for 10–15 minutes or until very tender (insert the point of a sharp knife into the stems to test). Drain and purée to a smooth consistency, adding extra liquid if necessary.

GREEN BEAN

The thinner varieties of green beans are best for this purée, as they tend to be less stringy . If you are able to obtain only large beans, you will need to cook them longer and strain the purée before serving.

5 crisp green beans

Wash the beans thoroughly, then top and tail. Steam them for 10–15 minutes or until tender and almost wilted. Purée until smooth, adding extra liquid as necessary.

CAULIFLOWER & BROCCOLI

Cauliflower and broccoli have a natural affinity and together produce a pretty green purée which is as harmonious to the eye as it is to the palate.

MAKES 6 PORTIONS

3–4 cauliflower flowerets
3–4 broccoli flowerets

Wash the vegetables well. Place them in a saucepan of boiling water. Cover and simmer for 10–15 minutes, until the point of a sharp knife can be inserted easily into the stems. Drain and purée, adding extra liquid as necessary.

CARROT, PARSNIP & RUTABAGA

Since most babies love root vegetables, this falls into the rare "fail-safe" category.

MAKES 8 PORTIONS

1 medium carrot, peeled, and diced
1 medium parsnip, peeled, and diced
½-inch slice medium rutabaga, peeled, and diced

Place the prepared vegetables in a saucepan of boiling water. Cover and simmer for 25–30 minutes (depending on the age of the vegetables) until very tender. Drain and purée to a smooth consistency, adding extra liquid as necessary.

GREEN BEAN & RED PEPPER

The natural sweetness of red peppers makes beans more interesting.

MAKES 6 PORTIONS

5 green beans, rinsed, trimmed, and chopped
½ red pepper, rinsed, seeded, and chopped

Place the beans in a saucepan of boiling water. Cover and simmer for 5 minutes. Add the chopped pepper and simmer for 5 minutes longer. Drain and purée, adding extra liquid as necessary.

POTATO, LEEK & SPINACH

The taste of onion can be a little overpowering for babies, and its effect on immature digestive systems can be dramatic. Leek is a subtler alternative.

MAKES 10 PORTIONS

1 *medium potato, scrubbed, peeled, and diced*
1 *tender young leek, thoroughly rinsed, trimmed, and chopped*
5 *fresh spinach leaves, rinsed, stems removed, and chopped*

Place the potato and leek in a saucepan of boiling water. Cover and simmer until very tender, about 20 minutes. Drain. Meanwhile, place the prepared spinach leaves (with the water adhering to them after washing) in another saucepan over low heat. Simmer gently for 5 minutes or until tender. Drain and purée with the potato and leek, adding extra liquid as necessary.

CELERY ROOT & POTATO

This makes a delicious purée, which is loved just as much by adults.

MAKES 8 PORTIONS

1-*inch slice celery root, scrubbed, peeled, and chopped*
1 *medium potato, scrubbed, peeled, and chopped*

Place the celery root and potato in a saucepan of boiling water. Cover and simmer until tender, 20–30 minutes. Drain and mash to a smooth purée (using a fork), adding breast or formula milk to give the required consistency.

ZUCCHINI & CARROT

Combining carrots with zucchini made me feel better about serving them so frequently!

MAKES 8 PORTIONS

1 *medium carrot, scrubbed, peeled, and trimmed*
1 *small zucchini, rinsed and trimmed*

Dice the carrot and zucchini. Add the diced carrot to a saucepan of boiling water, cover, and simmer for about 15 minutes. Add the zucchini and continue cooking for 10–15 minutes longer. Drain the vegetables and purée to a smooth consistency. The zucchini is very watery, so you should not need to add extra liquid.

PARSNIP & APPLE

Fruit and vegetable combinations often work, but this is especially successful.

MAKES 8 PORTIONS

1 small young parsnip
1 small apple

Scrub, trim away the root and tip, and peel the parsnip. Cut into quarters, core, and dice. Wash, peel, core, and chop the apple. Place the parsnip pieces in a saucepan of boiling water, cover, and simmer for 15 minutes. Add the apple and continue cooking for 5–10 minutes longer. Drain and purée to a smooth consistency, adding extra liquid as necessary.

APPLE & PEAR

Another "fail-safe" combination, this makes a great freezer standby.

MAKES 6–8 PORTIONS

1 small apple, rinsed, peeled,
cored, and chopped
1 small ripe pear, rinsed, peeled, cored, and chopped

Place the fruit in a saucepan with a little water. Bring to a boil, cover, and simmer for 5–8 minutes or until tender. Purée to a smooth consistency, adding extra liquid as necessary.

PRUNE & APPLE

This preserves the flavor of the prunes, while counteracting their side effects.

MAKES 8–10 PORTIONS

Mix together one recipe Apple Purée and one recipe Prune Purée (see pages 23–4).

APRICOT & PEACH

Not so much a purée as a nectar.

MAKES 8 PORTIONS

Mix together one recipe Apricot Purée and one recipe Peach Purée (see pages 23–4). For slightly older babies, add a little yogurt.

AVOCADO & PEAR

The sweet/savory contrast makes this combination very successful.

MAKES 1 PORTION

½-inch slice ripe avocado
½-inch slice very ripe pear, peeled

Mash the avocado and pear together until smooth and well combined. For older babies, add a little cottage cheese to the mixture for extra protein.

FOUR TO SIX MONTHS MENU CHART

Use this Menu Chart as a guide only. You can substitute any of the purée recipes for those suggested here, as long as you introduce one food at a time, and let your baby dictate the pace.

INGREDIENTS CHECKLIST*

Apples
Carrots
Rice

Week 1&2	Early Morning	Breakfast	Lunch	Dinner	Bedtime
Day 1	Milk	Milk	Milk Baby Rice	Milk	Milk
Day 2	Milk	Milk	Milk Baby Rice	Milk	Milk
Day 3	Milk	Milk	Milk Baby Rice	Milk	Milk
Day 4	Milk	Milk	Milk Apple Purée	Milk	Milk
Day 5	Milk	Milk	Milk Apple Purée	Milk	Milk
Day 6	Milk	Milk	Milk Apple Purée	Milk	Milk
Day 7	Milk	Milk	Milk Carrot Purée	Milk	Milk

NB In this and subsequent Menu Charts, recipes contained in this book are indicated in bold type.

* Use this Ingredients Checklist and those in later chapters to help you shop, depending on the preferences of your baby and how closely you decide to follow the Menu Charts (basic store-cupboard ingredients are not included).

FOUR TO SIX MONTHS MENU CHART *cont.*

After a week or so, your baby will be ready to progress to two solid feedings a day, and you can begin to vary the diet from day to day.

INGREDIENTS CHECKLIST

Avocados
Bananas
Parsnips
Peaches
Pears
Potatoes
Rice
Zucchini

Week 3	Early Morning	Breakfast	Lunch	Dinner	Bedtime
Day 1	Milk	Milk Baby Rice	Milk Zucchini Purée	Milk	Milk
Day 2	Milk	Milk Baby Rice	Milk Pear Purée	Milk	Milk
Day 3	Milk	Milk Baby Rice	Milk Potato Purée	Milk	Milk
Day 4	Milk	Milk Baby Rice	Milk Mashed Banana	Milk	Milk
Day 5	Milk	Milk Baby Rice	Milk Parsnip Purée	Milk	Milk
Day 6	Milk	Milk Baby Rice	Milk Peach Purée	Milk	Milk
Day 7	Milk	Milk Baby Rice	Milk Mashed Avocado	Milk	Milk

FOUR TO SIX MONTHS MENU CHART *cont.*

*Towards the **end** of the first month of weaning, your baby will be ready for three "meals" a day, though of course these will still be just small tasters.*

INGREDIENTS
CHECKLIST

Apples
Apricots
Avocados
Bananas
Carrots
Cauliflower
Green beans
Mango
Melon
Pears
Potatoes
Prunes
Rice
Sweet potatoes

Week 4	Early Morning	Breakfast	Lunch	Dinner	Bedtime
Day 1	Milk	Milk Baby Rice	Sweet Potato Purée Milk	Apricot Purée Milk	Milk
Day 2	Milk	Milk Baby Rice	Cauliflower Purée Milk	Prune Purée Milk	Milk
Day 3	Milk	Milk Baby Rice	Green Bean Purée Milk	Melon Purée Milk	Milk
Day 4	Milk	Milk Baby Rice	Carrot Purée Pear Purée Water Milk	Mashed Banana Milk	Milk
Day 5	Milk	Milk Baby Rice	Potato Purée Prune Purée Water Milk	Apple Purée Milk	Milk
Day 6	Milk	Milk Baby Rice	Cauliflower Purée Pear Purée Water Milk	Mango Purée Milk	Milk
Day 7	Milk	Milk Baby Rice	Avocado Purée Melon Purée Water Milk	Mashed Banana Milk	Milk

FOUR TO SIX MONTHS MENU CHART *cont.*

Your baby's appetite for solids and larger quantities should now be firmly established. You can now safely combine fruits and vegetables to make more interesting purées.

INGREDIENTS CHECKLIST

Apples
Apricots
Avocados
Baby cereal
Bananas
Broccoli
Carrots
Cauliflower
Celery root
Green beans
Leeks
Mango
Melon
Parsnips
Peaches
Pears
Peas
Potatoes
Prunes
Red pepper
Rutabaga
Spinach
Zucchini

Week 5&6	Early Morning	Breakfast	Lunch	Dinner	Bedtime
Day 1	Milk	Mashed Banana Milk	Carrot, Parsnip & Rutabaga Purée Melon Purée Boiled water	Mashed Avocado Milk	Milk
Day 2	Milk	Baby cereal Milk	Celery Root & Potato Purée Prune Purée Boiled water	Mashed Banana Milk	Milk
Day 3	Milk	Apple & Pear Purée Milk	Cauliflower & Broccoli Purée Peach Purée Boiled water	Zucchini Purée Milk	Milk
Day 4	Milk	Baby cereal Milk	Parsnip & Apple Purée Apricot Purée Boiled water	Prune & Apple Purée Milk	Milk
Day 5	Milk	Mashed Banana Milk	Potato, Leek & Spinach Purée Apple & Pear Purée Boiled water	Carrot Purée Milk	Milk
Day 6	Milk	Baby cereal Milk	Green Bean & Red Pepper Purée Prune Purée Boiled water	Peach Purée Milk	Milk
Day 7	Milk	Mango Purée Milk	Zucchini & Carrot Purée Banana	Avocado & Pear Purée Milk	Milk

CHAPTER THREE

Texture & Taste

SIX TO NINE MONTHS

Somewhere between the ages of six and nine months, most babies enter what experts and health professionals term the second stage of weaning. Broadly speaking, this means the stage when they are able to tolerate proteins (other than milk) and gluten and cope with some texture in their food. This can be the beginning of a short honeymoon phase when it comes to feeding your child (though some do become fussy at this time). Over the next few months your baby will probably establish a fairly regular eating pattern, gain weight rapidly, enjoy something approximating three meals a day, and display few fussy feeding habits. Although most babies are more than content with a fairly monotonous diet, make the most of this phase while it lasts to introduce as many new flavors and textures as possible. You'll be doing both yourself and your child a great service in the long run.

At this age, milk still plays a major role in your baby's diet, but milk alone is no longer nutritionally adequate. The iron stores your baby was born with are depleting and the rapid growth rate means that extra protein, vitamins, minerals, and calories are required. You should still make sure your baby has sufficient milk in addition to solid food (approximately 24 ounces of breast or formula milk per day at eight months). This amount of milk is necessary for the continued healthy development of bones and teeth.

Whether you give breast or formula milk is entirely a matter of personal choice, although cow's milk should not be introduced (other than in cooking) until your baby is at least one year old (after this time limit milk to 1 quart per day). If you have breast-fed your baby during the first few months and now for reasons of convenience (perhaps because of a return to work) you decide to opt for bottles instead, do not feel guilty. The major advantages of breast feeding are already confirmed, such as increased resistance to disease as a result of receiving maternal antibodies. Some mothers find they can happily continue feeding at bedtime only for an indefinite time, so, if this suits you and your baby, by all means continue. I found that once I switched to bottles during the day my milk supply rapidly dried up.

To prevent your hungry baby from being overly frustrated when you are trying to introduce solids, give a little milk first, then switch to very small half-spoonfuls of food, and finally finish off with more milk if need be. Once solid feeding is well established, do not offer your baby milk during meals. If your baby is thirsty before or during mealtimes, offer very weak fruit juice or, preferably, cooled, boiled water. Always give your baby juice in a training cup, never a bottle, to minimize the risk of damage from sugars and acids associated with sucking on a bottle. Although the sugars naturally present in fruit juice are preferable to artificial sugars, your baby's delicate new teeth, which are being formed at this time, can't tell the difference (the acids in many commercial drinks and fruit juices could also be harmful to teeth). And don't be seduced by the commercial herbal drinks. Ignore the hype, read the label, and reject anything containing a high proportion of "oses," that is, fructose, sucrose, and lactose, which are just sugar in scientific clothing. Avoid artificial sweeteners such as saccharin and aspartame, found in sugar-free beverages and some yogurts (they are prohibited from being added to baby foods).

TOWARD THREE MEALS

Once your baby has come to grips with solid food you will find that he or she soon learns to enjoy regular mealtimes. Now that gluten (found in wheat products like bread and cereals) is no longer a problem, cereals together with some form of fruit are an excellent choice for breakfast. Despite the marketing pressure on parents to purchase special baby cereals, a box of oatmeal, preferably organic, and a box of whole-wheat rusks or crackers are all you need for a healthy start to your baby's day.

At this age it is best to make lunch the main meal of the day, and this is also the time to introduce new foods. Your baby is most likely to be receptive in the middle of the day and, in the unlikely event of one food having a disagreeable effect, there is time to deal with the consequences before bedtime.

And, it is worth mentioning that much of what goes in will come out in a recognizable form. (I offer this reassurance so you do not repeat my experience of rushing my baby and his alarming diaper to the emergency room, to be greeted by hoots of derision.)

Remember, too, that appetite can exceed ability at this age. When my son Krishnan was nine months old, we took a vacation in France and were delighted to be able to take him out to restaurants with us where he would happily suck on a hunk of baguette while we enjoyed dinner. After several days he began to refuse food and we discovered a huge wad of pulped bread welded to the roof of his mouth! In other words, babies will, quite literally, bite off more than they can chew. For this reason, they should never be left unattended while eating.

GENERAL GUIDELINES

Most fruits and vegetables are now acceptable but they should still be rinsed, peeled, and, where appropriate (for example, grapes, tomatoes), seeded. Wheat-based foods and citrus fruits may be offered from seven months. You may now also introduce cheese and, at seven to eight months, eggs, but avoid soft and blue cheeses, and use only the yolks of eggs, since egg white is still difficult for your baby to digest. Eggs must be hard-boiled to kill any salmonella or other bacteria. Introduce legumes as an alternative source of protein, but make the process gradual, and mash them or they will pass through your baby's digestive system undigested. Mash beans or lentils with a little oil to make them more palatable and add essential calories. Never be afraid to add a good-quality vegetable oil, such as olive oil, soybean oil, or walnut oil, to home-prepared baby foods, particularly for vegetarian babies who are not consuming fat in animal foods.

You can, and should, begin to introduce moderate amounts of herbs and spices as flavorings at this stage, and I recommend this wherever possible if you don't wish to end up with a fussy toddler who views every unidentified fleck with suspicion. The only absolute seasoning taboo is salt. Until your baby is at least one year old the kidneys will be too immature to deal with it. Since many of the recipes which follow are suitable for the whole family, I suggest you isolate your baby's portion before seasoning your own.

TEXTURE

In the parental interests of trouble-free, fast feeding, it is all too tempting to continue puréeing your baby's food to a spoonable mush indefinitely. In a word, don't, or you will end up with one of those infuriating infants who rejects every piece of fruit in yogurt and lines up on the side of the plate every chunk of vegetable more than a fraction of an inch square. Begin by mashing rather than puréeing food, and don't worry if at first your baby gags and spits a little. Babies quickly get the hang of chewing, even if they don't have many, or any, teeth. Gums are remarkably efficient at pulverizing well-cooked vegetables. Toast strips, rusks, cubes of cheese, and steamed crudités are all ways of introducing interesting textures and the mechanics of mastication. Remember that, though the risks of choking on such foods are very low, children of this age should always be supervised while eating.

QUANTITIES

Each recipe in this book gives the number of portions produced, but this is always approximate. Each individual baby's appetite is the only infallible guide to quantity. I have come across babies built like small sumo wrestlers who happily toy with a couple of teaspoons of food at every meal and continue to thrive. My advice is to offer your baby a little to begin with, and keep going until interest seems to have waned. Provided your baby continues to gain weight and make good progress, you can rest assured that all is well.

PRACTICALITIES

Make sure your baby is comfortable before attempting to feed. At around six months, most babies are taking their meals in a bouncy chair or on your lap; toward the end of this phase they have usually progressed to a high chair. Try to maintain a calm, relaxed atmosphere and never force your baby to eat. Like you, sometimes he or she will be genuinely hungry, but at other times food may not be needed.

Never serve a baby hot food; always cool it to lukewarm. If you use a microwave to reheat your baby's food, always leave the food to stand for a minute or so, and check the temperature in the middle (the outside can be scalding while the inside remains cool). Most babies seem to prefer the feel of plastic rather than metal spoons in their mouths and, of course, everything tastes better sucked from their own fists. Hard plastic bibs are practical, but some children, my own son included, find their rigidity claustrophobic. In this case, try compromising with a vinyl-lined cotton bib. Above all, try to make feeding your baby a special time to share rather than a chore.

SOUPS AND DIPS

Parsnip & Apple Soup

Fruit and root combinations readily appeal to palates still attuned to the natural sweetness of breast milk. To make a thicker, more substantial purée, simply reduce the amount of vegetable stock and milk.

MAKES 12 PORTIONS

1 tablespoon butter
5 cups peeled and
roughly chopped parsnips
1 large apple, peeled, cored, and roughly
chopped

pinch of dried sage (optional)
1 quart unsalted vegetable stock
⅔ cup yogurt

Melt the butter and gently cook the parsnips and apple for 10 minutes or until soft. Sprinkle the sage (if using) on the parsnips and apple, then stir in the stock. Bring to a boil and simmer for 30–40 minutes or until the vegetables are very tender. Allow the soup to cool slightly, then purée. Return to the pan, add the yogurt and reheat gently.

| ☺ | ☹ | ❄ |

Ten-minute Tomato Soup

Most children's love affair with tomato soup begins in babyhood, so this quicker-than-opening-a-can version is a great standby. My son has adored this since he was tiny, and it is still his favorite "sick food," slipping down a sore throat when all else fails to tempt. For healthy infants, serve with fingers of dry toast or bread-sticks, which they can dip into the soup themselves while you take charge of the spoon.

MAKES 12 PORTIONS

1 *cup pure strained tomatoes, such as Pomi*
2½ cups milk, or

mixture of milk and light cream
pinch of sugar, or to taste

Heat the strained tomatoes gently, stir in the milk, or milk and cream mixture, bring to a boil and let simmer gently for 5 minutes. Add a little sugar to taste.

Crudités

Crudités are a good way of introducing your baby to different textures and the idea of chewing as a useful aid to eating, rather than just a means of exploration! Although at this age very little of the vegetables will actually be consumed, they will ease the soreness of teething gums while helping to develop your child's burgeoning sense of independence, and feeding skills.

Celery pieces, lightly steamed
Carrot pieces, lightly steamed
Flowerets of cauliflower and broccoli,
lightly steamed

Green beans, lightly steamed
Snow peas, lightly steamed
Baby ears of corn, lightly steamed
Avocado slices

Vegetables served in this way should be washed thoroughly, peeled, cut into manageable pieces (small enough for tiny fists to grip, yet large enough to prevent your baby from swallowing them whole and choking), and lightly steamed. I have found the varieties above are particularly well-received. Serve them with a nutritious dip (see the suggestions on the following pages) for a tasty treat.

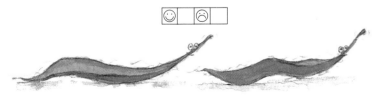

Avocado & Cottage Cheese Dip

Babies love the creamy, smooth texture of avocado as well as its unchallenging taste. Make this dip as close to mealtime as possible, since the avocado flesh will discolor. If you have to prepare it in advance, placing the pit in the bowl helps to prevent discoloration. The recipe gives enough to make an adult dip as well—just add seasoning and a dash of hot-pepper sauce.

MAKES 4–6 PORTIONS

1 *medium-sized, ripe avocado*   ½ *cup cottage cheese*

Cut the avocado in half, remove the pit, and place the flesh in the bowl of a food processor. Add the cottage cheese. Blend until smooth.

Happy Hummus

Commercial hummus contains a great deal of salt, which is undesirable for young babies. This version retains all the goodness without the unwanted extra salt.

MAKES 6 PORTIONS

15-*oz can chick peas (garbanzo beans),*   4 *tablespoons tahini (sesame-seed paste)*
drained and rinsed   *juice of ½ lemon*
½ *clove garlic, peeled and crushed*   *a little plain yogurt*

Place the chick peas (garbanzo beans), garlic, tahini, and lemon juice in the bowl of a food processor. Blend until smooth, adding a little yogurt to the mixture to achieve the required consistency.

Creamy Cheese Dip

Mild and mollifying, this simple dip is especially enjoyable with chunks of apple, pineapple, or pear to plunge into it.

MAKES 4 PORTIONS

2 oz mild cheddar or Colby cheese, grated (½ cup)

2 tablespoons plain yogurt
1 tablespoon butter, softened

Place the grated cheese, yogurt and softened butter in a bowl. Beat together until smooth and creamy.

Magic Mushroom Mush

I call this magic not because it incorporates hallucinogenic fungi (though at the end of a trying day parents may well wish it did), but because many small children have a built-in aversion to mushrooms, and, prepared in this way, they seem to become magically acceptable. Try this as a sandwich filling as well as a dip.

MAKES 8–10 PORTIONS

1 tablespoon olive oil
1 small onion, finely chopped
3 cups wiped and
finely chopped mushrooms

½ clove garlic, peeled and crushed
2 tablespoons finely chopped parsley
2 cups canned cannellini beans, drained
and rinsed

Heat the oil and gently cook the onion until soft, about 10 minutes. Add the mushrooms, garlic, and parsley and continue to cook for about 15 minutes, until soft. Place the cooked vegetables in the bowl of a food processor, together with the cannellini beans, and blend until smooth. Chill before serving.

SANDWICHES AND RUSKS

Tiny sandwiches make great finger food. At this age, like most babies, Krishnan preferred white bread to whole-wheat and, though white bread has a lower fiber content, on a vegetarian diet this is not a problem. The following filling suggestions were his favorites.

Grated Cheese with
Apple Butter

Apple butter is available at many health food stores. Because it is made entirely from fruit, it has the sweetness which babies love without the added sugar.

MAKES 2 SANDWICHES OR MORE FINGERS

2 *thin slices white bread*
1 *teaspoon butter, softened*

1 *teaspoon apple butter*
1 *oz mild cheddar cheese, grated (¼ cup)*

Spread the bread sparingly with butter, then the apple butter. Top one slice with grated cheese, sandwich together, and cut into small fingers.

☺ ☹

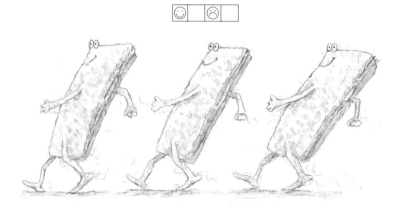

Cream Cheese & Pineapple

Use full-fat cream cheese for babies, since calorie requirements outweigh cholesterol concerns at this age. Vary this combination by replacing the pineapple with peeled and chopped peaches or mashed banana.

MAKES 2 SANDWICHES OR MORE FINGERS

1 *tablespoon cream cheese*
½-inch slice fresh pineapple, peeled and cored

2 *thin slices white bread*

Place the cream cheese and pineapple in the bowl of a food processor and blend until smooth. Spread the bread with this mixture, then sandwich together. Cut into quarters or fingers, or use a small cookie cutter to stamp out interesting shapes.

Egg & Tomato

Egg white is unsuitable for babies of this age because the proteins it contains are too complex for their digestive systems, but the yolk is a valuable source of both digestible protein and energy.

MAKES 2 SANDWICHES OR MORE FINGERS/SHAPES

1 *free-range egg*
2 *thin slices white bread*
1 *teaspoon butter, softened*

1 *tablespoon plain yogurt*
1 *tomato, peeled, seeded, and finely chopped* (*see opposite*)

Hard-boil the egg for 12 minutes, then drain and cover with cold water. Peel the egg, and discard the shell and egg white. Spread the bread with the softened butter. Mash the yolk with the yogurt. Spread the egg and yogurt mixture on the bread, sprinkle the tomato over the top, and sandwich the bread together. Cut the sandwiches into fingers or shapes.

Pink Panther Spread

This deliciously creamy mixture has a lovely delicate pink hue which babies find appealing. The recipe gives enough to make the extra into a spread for adults—just add seasoning and mustard.

MAKES 2 SANDWICHES OR MORE FINGERS/SHAPES

7-*oz can butter beans, drained and rinsed*
2 *tomatoes*

1 *teaspoon butter, softened*
2 *thin slices white bread*

Place the drained beans in the bowl of a food processor. Peel the tomatoes (to make this easier, make an incision in the shape of a cross on the top of the tomato and plunge into boiling water for 1–2 minutes). Remove the tomato seeds using a pointed teaspoon, and chop the flesh. Add the tomato to the beans and blend to a smooth purée. Spread the butter on the bread, then spoon the bean-and-tomato mixture on the bread and sandwich together. Cut the sandwiches into fingers or shapes.

Rusks

All babies love to gnaw on rusks, which also make a good breakfast cereal if crumbled into breast or formula milk. Making your own rusks is actually very easy and highly rewarding because they taste so much better (and usually have less sugar) than commercial varieties.

MAKES 36 RUSKS

3¼ cups white bread flour
2 teaspoons cream of tartar
1 teaspoon baking soda
⅓ cup sugar

1 stick butter, chilled
1 large free-range egg, beaten
1 cup buttermilk

Sift the flour, cream of tartar, and baking soda together. Stir in the sugar. Cut in the butter until the mixture resembles fine bread crumbs.

Mix together the egg and buttermilk, then add this to the flour mixture and knead lightly until the mixture forms a soft ball. Using your hands, pat the dough evenly into an oiled 13 x 8-inch jelly roll pan. Mark into 36 fingers using a sharp knife. Bake at 400°F for 30 minutes. Remove the rusks from the oven, cut them into slices, and arrange them on baking sheets. Lower the heat to 250°F and return the rusks to the oven until dry. When cool, store the rusks in an airtight container.

French Toast

In our house, any pretensions to gracious living are relentlessly quashed by my four-year-old, who persists in referring to one of his favorite baby breakfasts as "eggy bread." Nowadays he enjoys it with ketchup, but then, with a mindful eye to salt and sugar levels, I used to serve it with tomato paste.

MAKES 2 PORTIONS

1 *free-range egg, beaten*
1 *thick slice white bread*

a little butter for frying

Beat the egg and pour it into a shallow dish. Soak both sides of the bread in the egg. Melt the butter in a small skillet and slowly fry the egg-soaked bread on both sides until golden and crispy. Slice into fingers.

HEARTY HELPINGS

Macaroni & Cheese

As a baby, my son enjoyed macaroni and cheese so much, he would, if allowed, have eaten it practically every day. For variety, try adding a few frozen peas and/or some corn to the cheese sauce.

MAKES 10 PORTIONS

¾ cup macaroni
2 tablespoons butter
¼ cup all-purpose flour

1¼ cups milk
3 oz mild cheddar cheese, grated (¼ cup)
1 tablespoon dry bread crumbs

Cook the macaroni according to the directions on the package. Drain. Melt the butter in a pan, add the flour, and cook without browning for 2 minutes. Using a balloon whisk, gradually incorporate the milk into the flour and butter mixture until a smooth sauce forms. Simmer the sauce for a couple of minutes, then remove from the heat and stir in two-thirds of the grated cheese.

Stir the cooked macaroni into the cheese sauce until it is well coated. Transfer to a shallow gratin dish. Mix the remaining cheese with the bread crumbs, then sprinkle over the macaroni. Place under a pre-heated broiler until golden brown and bubbling.

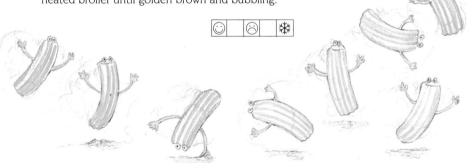

Napolitana Pasta Sauce

This quick, simple-to-make sauce can be used as the basis for many dishes. Add variety by including vegetables and/or cheese, according to your baby's preferences. Or serve on potato gnocchi instead of with pasta.

MAKES 6 PORTIONS

2 teaspoons olive oil
½ clove garlic, peeled and crushed
2 teaspoons chopped fresh basil

2 teaspoons chopped fresh flat-leaf parsley
14-oz can crushed tomatoes

Heat the oil, add the garlic and herbs, and cook lightly for 2 minutes. Stir in the tomatoes and simmer, uncovered, for about 15 minutes, until the sauce reduces and thickens (continue stirring to break up the tomato). Serve with pasta shapes.

Hummus Pasta Sauce

This takes only minutes to prepare, so it is ideal for the frequent occasions when time is at a premium.

MAKES 6 PORTIONS

2 teaspoons olive oil
2 scallions, finely chopped

4 tablespoons Hummus
(see page 40)
1–2 tablespoons milk

Heat the oil in a saucepan and gently cook the scallions until soft and golden. Stir in the hummus and enough milk to make a smooth, saucelike consistency. Simmer gently for 5–10 minutes, stirring. Serve with tiny pasta shapes.

Sweet Pepper Pasta Sauce

Red peppers are extremely rich in vitamin C, which helps the iron in the parsley to be absorbed by the body. Fortunately, this sauce tastes good too!

MAKES 6 PORTIONS

2 teaspoons olive oil
2 red peppers, seeded and chopped
½ small onion, peeled and chopped
¼ clove garlic, peeled and finely chopped

¼ cup canned crushed tomatoes
2 teaspoons chopped fresh parsley
pinch of sugar

Heat the oil, add the peppers, onion, garlic, and tomatoes, and stew gently for 15–20 minutes or until very tender. Stir in the parsley and season with the sugar. Cook for 2–3 minutes longer. Blend to a smooth sauce in a food processor.

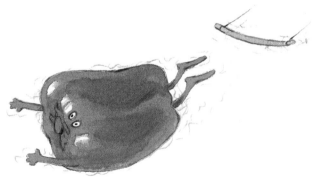

Fruity Couscous

Remember to wash the dried fruit thoroughly before using, as many brands are coated with sulfur dioxide to keep them bright and plump.

MAKES 10 PORTIONS

¼ cup dried apricots
⅓ cup raisins
2 tablespoons canned coconut milk

1 tablespoon turbinado sugar
½ teaspoon cinnamon
⅔ cup couscous

Chop the apricots and place in a saucepan with the raisins. Add enough water to cover. Bring to a boil and simmer for about 10 minutes or until tender.

Mix the coconut with water to make 1¼ cups. Stir in the sugar and cinnamon. Transfer the coconut mixture to a saucepan and gradually bring to a boil, stirring, until the sugar dissolves. Stir the couscous into the coconut, remove from the heat, and cover. Let stand for 3–5 minutes, until all the water is absorbed. Fluff up the couscous using a fork. Drain the dried fruit and stir it into the couscous.

Khichri

My son's father is from the Indian state of Gujarat, where this dish is a staple infant food. True to his genetic heritage, Krishnan loved it from his first spoonful.

MAKES 10 PORTIONS

¼ cup split red lentils
1 sliver of garlic
1 sliver of gingerroot, peeled
½ bay leaf

1 tomato, peeled, seeded, and finely chopped
⅓ cup basmati rice
1–2 tablespoons plain yogurt

Thoroughly rinse and pick over the lentils. Place in a saucepan with the garlic, ginger, and bay leaf. Cover with water and bring to a boil, then simmer for 40–50 minutes or until very tender, adding extra water if required (the cooked lentils should be the consistency of a thick soup). Discard the ginger, garlic, and bay leaf. Add the chopped tomato and continue cooking for 5 minutes longer.

Meanwhile, rinse the rice under plenty of running water and cook according to the directions on the package until tender. Drain. Combine the rice with the lentil mixture and stir in the yogurt. For younger babies, purée the mixture.

Spring Vegetable Risotto

Rice is always popular with babies, and the lovely bright greens of the vegetables in this dish are very appealing to small eyes.

MAKES 6–8 PORTIONS

8 oz mixed green vegetables, such as young peas, zucchini, fava beans
knob of butter
1 teaspoon olive oil

3 scallions, finely chopped
¾ cup arborio rice
2 cups vegetable stock
½ teaspoon dried oregano

Prepare the green vegetables and steam them for 8–10 minutes or until tender. Melt the butter with the oil, add the scallions, and cook until soft. Add the rice to the scallions and stir well. Continue cooking gently until the rice is opaque but not brown.

Add about one-third of the stock to the rice and continue cooking over low heat until the stock is absorbed, about 10 minutes. Add another third of the stock, along with the cooked vegetables and oregano, and continue cooking until the liquid is absorbed. Add the remaining stock and let the rice continue simmering until it is quite tender and all the liquid has been absorbed. For younger babies, purée the mixture before serving.

Broccoli & Cauliflower with Cheese Sauce

This is a colorful variation of either broccoli or cauliflower alone with cheese. For a more substantial dish, add a handful of cooked pasta shapes to the sauce with the vegetables.

MAKES 12 PORTIONS

6 oz cauliflower flowerets
6 oz broccoli flowerets
CHEESE SAUCE
2 tablespoons butter

2 tablespoons all-purpose flour
vegetable liquid plus milk to make 1¼ cups
4 oz mild cheddar or Gruyère cheese, grated (1 cup)

Rinse the vegetables and boil quickly in a small amount of water until tender but not watery, about 10 minutes. Reserve the liquid. Meanwhile, prepare the cheese sauce: melt the butter, stir in the flour, and cook over low heat for 1–2 minutes, stirring constantly. Gradually whisk in the vegetable liquid and milk, continuing until the sauce is thick. Remove from the heat, stir in the grated cheese and add the vegetables. Purée in a food processor or blender, or mash coarsely with a fork.

Cheese & Potato Bake

This is one of the staples at my son's preschool, where they have apparently never come across a child who doesn't love it. Among older children, it is even more popular when baked beans appear as an accompaniment. I generally use cheddar cheese, but Gruyère or Gouda can be used for variety.

MAKES 8–10 PORTIONS

1 lb baking potatoes, peeled
a little butter and milk for mashing

⅔ cup cottage cheese
4 oz cheddar cheese, grated (1 cup)

Boil the potatoes in unsalted water until tender. Drain and mash them to a smooth consistency with a little butter and milk. Stir in the cottage cheese and half the grated cheddar. Pile the mixture into a shallow gratin dish and sprinkle the remaining cheddar over the top. Place under a preheated broiler until the cheese melts and is golden.

Ratatouille

My son used to adore ratatouille mixed with mashed potato and sprinkled with grated cheese. Pasta shapes or boiled rice are also good accompaniments.

MAKES 8–10 PORTIONS

salt
1 large eggplant, sliced
2 zucchini, sliced
2 tablespoons olive oil
1 large onion, peeled and chopped

1 clove garlic, peeled and finely chopped
½ green pepper, seeded and chopped
½ red pepper, seeded and chopped
8-oz can crushed tomatoes
1 tablespoon chopped basil

Sprinkle salt on the eggplant and zucchini slices, then place them in a colander and cover with a heavy weight. Leave for 30 minutes to let all the bitter juices drain off. Rinse thoroughly, dry on paper towels and chop.

Heat the oil, add the onion and cook gently until soft but not brown. Add the garlic, eggplant, zucchini, and peppers. Cover and cook slowly for about 30 minutes or until tender. Finally, stir in the tomatoes and basil and simmer, uncovered, for 30 minutes longer. For younger babies, purée the mixture before serving.

Bubble & Squeak

This traditional English dish, said to be named for the sound the mixture makes while cooking, seems to be one of the few ways of preparing cabbage acceptable to babies. For toddlers, form the mixture into small patties and fry until crispy and golden to serve with vegetarian sausages or burgers. Let your child hear the mixture cooking—it really does live up to its name.

MAKES 8–10 PORTIONS

12 oz baking potatoes
12 oz young cabbage
1 leek, rinsed and very finely chopped

¼ cup milk
knob of butter

Peel and dice the potatoes, then boil for about 20 minutes, or until tender. Meanwhile, thoroughly rinse the cabbage, discarding any dark, bitter leaves, and cutting out any tough pieces of stem. Shred the leaves finely and steam for about 20 minutes, or until very tender. Poach the leek in the milk until soft, about 10 minutes. Mash the potatoes with the leek and milk mixture, add a little butter and stir in the cabbage.

☺ ☹ ❄

Spinach, Potato & Leek Curry

Don't be perturbed by the idea of feeding your baby curry. This very delicately spiced dish has no chilies and is as far removed from a spicy vindaloo as flocked wallpaper is from frescoes. As a result of introducing Krishnan to a moderate amount of spice at an early age, he has always been decidedly less intimidated by new flavors than many of his peers.

MAKES 12 PORTIONS

10 oz frozen leaf spinach
1 tablespoon vegetable oil
½ cup finely chopped leek
1 clove garlic, peeled and finely chopped
1½ cups peeled and cubed potatoes

1 medium tomato, peeled, seeded, and finely chopped
1 tablespoon plain yogurt
¼ teaspoon garam masala or mild curry powder

Cook the frozen spinach according to the directions on the package. Drain, squeezing out as much water as you can, then chop finely in a food processor. Heat the oil, add the leek and garlic—cook until soft. Add the potatoes, spinach, and tomato—cook for 2 minutes. Stir in the yogurt and continue cooking until a creamy consistency forms. Add a little water, cover, and simmer until the potatoes are very tender. Sprinkle the garam masala onto the vegetable mixture, cook for 5 minutes longer, then mash or purée according to the age of your baby. Serve with fingers of plain naan or pita bread (most supermarkets sell these flat breads), or rice, and a little plain yogurt.

Lentil Sambhar

Most babies love the nutty sweetness of coconut, which in this dish combines beautifully with the fresh flavors of the vegetables.

MAKES 12 PORTIONS

½ cup red lentils, rinsed and picked over
½ clove garlic, peeled and finely sliced
1 thin slice gingerroot, peeled
4 oz mixed vegetables (such as cauliflower flowerets, green beans, and potatoes)

1 medium tomato, peeled, seeded, and chopped
1 oz flaked coconut

Place the lentils in a pan with the garlic and ginger. Cover with water and bring to a boil, then simmer until very tender (30–40 minutes), adding extra water as required. Discard the gingerroot. Meanwhile, cut the vegetables into bite-size pieces and steam until tender. Add the tomato and coconut to the cooked lentils, stir well, bring to a boil, then simmer for 5–10 minutes longer. Stir the prepared vegetables into the lentils. Mash or purée to the desired consistency. Serve with rice.

Vegetable Goulash

Paprika is a very good spice to introduce at an early age, because babies seem to appreciate its piquant sweetness. For older babies, you can add a few caraway seeds for a more authentic flavor.

MAKES 12 PORTIONS

2 teaspoons vegetable oil
½ small onion, peeled and finely diced
1 small carrot, peeled and finely chopped
½ green pepper, peeled, seeded,
and finely chopped
½ red pepper, peeled, seeded,
and finely chopped
pinch mild paprika

1½ cups wiped and chopped mushrooms
1 medium potato, peeled and diced
2 tablespoons tomato paste
7-oz can red kidney beans, rinsed and
drained
⅔ cup basmati rice, cooked
1–2 tablespoons plain yogurt

Heat the oil, add the onion, carrot, peppers, and paprika, and cook slowly until soft but not brown. Add the mushrooms, cover, and continue cooking for 15 minutes. Add the potato, tomato paste and drained beans and let simmer for 30 minutes longer, or until the potato is very tender, adding a little extra water if required. Stir the rice into the cooked vegetables. Add the yogurt. Mash or purée to the desired consistency.

Zucchini Gratin

The creamy consistency of this delicately flavored vegetable dish never fails to please young gourmands. My son used to like it with a purée of garden peas or fava beans and some crusty French bread to dip in and suck. This recipe makes a large quantity and does not freeze well, so it is best for occasions when there are a few mouths to feed.

MAKES 10 PORTIONS

2 tablespoons butter
¼ cup all-purpose flour
1 cup milk
2 oz Swiss or Gruyère cheese, grated (½ cup)

pinch of grated nutmeg
1½ cups wiped and chopped zucchini
¾ cup fresh white bread crumbs

Melt the butter, stir in the flour, and cook, stirring continuously, for 2 minutes. Gradually blend in the milk, stirring until a smooth sauce forms. Remove from the heat, stir in the cheese and nutmeg, and leave to cool. Meanwhile, steam the zucchini for 5–10 minutes or until tender. Dry on paper towels, then stir into the cheese sauce. Transfer the mixture to a shallow gratin dish and sprinkle the bread crumbs over the top. Bake at 400°F for 15–20 minutes, or until bubbling and brown.

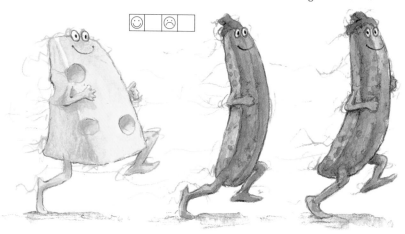

SWEET TREATS

Fruity Fool

I have used strawberries for this recipe because they are Krishnan's favorite, but you can try raspberries (strain the raspberry purée to remove the seeds) or blueberries, adding a little sugar or concentrated apple juice if the fruit is too tart. Prunes canned in fruit juice are also excellent.

MAKES 6 PORTIONS

1 pint strawberries, washed, hulled, and cooked

⅔ cup thick custard
⅔ cup plain yogurt

Purée the strawberries in a blender or food processor. Add the custard and yogurt and blend for about 30 seconds. Pour into individual dishes (ramekins are a good size) and chill thoroughly before serving.

Rice Pudding

Traditional rice pudding couldn't be easier to make, and babies love it warm or cold. The added evaporated milk in this recipe gives the pudding a delicious creamy richness. To vary the recipe, add a few rinsed dark or golden raisins, or chopped dried apricots.

MAKES 10 PORTIONS

2½ cups milk (use a 12-oz can of evaporated milk and make up the quantity with whole milk)

⅓ cup short-grain rice
2 tablespoons sugar
a little grated nutmeg (optional)

Grease a shallow 5-cup baking dish. Stir in the milk, rice, and sugar. Sprinkle the nutmeg over the top, if using. Cover with foil and bake in a preheated oven at 300°F for 2 hours.

Banana Oatmeal

Serve this either for breakfast or as a dessert. This recipe will freeze if the banana is left out, then added just before serving.

MAKES 4–6 PORTIONS

1¼ cups milk
⅓ cup oatmeal

1 small banana

Pour the milk into a saucepan, sprinkle the oatmeal into the milk, and bring to a boil, stirring all the time. Simmer for 1–2 minutes (or according to the instructions on the package) until creamy, then remove from the heat. Leave to cool. Mash the banana and stir it into the oatmeal until combined.

Juicy Gelatin

Gelatin is an easy food for your baby to eat and a great accompaniment to yogurt, cold custard, or ice cream. Commercial gelatins use as a setting agent a derivative of the boiled-down bones and hoofs of animal carcasses. This recipe uses agar-agar (available from health food stores) and fruit juice to make a healthy alternative.

MAKES 8 PORTIONS

1 *teaspoon agar-agar*
1¼ *cups fruit juice (pear, apple and rasp-berry, or apple and strawberry are all good)*

4 *oz finely chopped fresh fruit, such as bananas, kiwi fruit, peeled peaches, or strawberries (optional)*

D issolve the agar-agar according to the directions on the package and stir into the juice. Add the chopped fruit, if using. Pour the gelatin mixture into a 2½-cup mold or several individual molds. Chill until set.

Chocolate Pudding

Krishnan used to love this pudding with slices of ripe, peeled pear to dip into it.
Be warned, however—on the mess scale of 1–10, this dish rates 15!

MAKES 5 PORTIONS

*2 teaspoons high-quality unsweetened
cocoa powder*
1 teaspoon turbinado sugar

1 tablespoon cornstarch
1¼ cups milk

Dissolve the cocoa powder, sugar, and cornstarch in a little of the milk. Heat the remaining milk until almost boiling, then pour it onto the cocoa paste and stir well. Return the mixture to the pan and bring to a boil, stirring constantly until the mixture thickens. Leave to cool. Chill before serving.

Baby Muesli

Commercial baby cereals are often overpriced, and contain excessive amounts of refined sugar. The coconut in this muesli provides the sweetness babies enjoy, without empty calories. I soak the muesli in breast milk or formula milk overnight to give it a creamy consistency. You can add grated apple and chopped banana (and ground nuts, for older children) before serving to make it even more nutritious.

MAKES 8–10 PORTIONS

½ cup rolled oats
1 Weetabix cake

1 tablespoon flaked coconut

Place all the ingredients in a food processor and work to a fine powder. Store the prepared muesli in an airtight container.

SIX TO NINE MONTHS MENU CHART

Now that your baby is less reliant on milk feeds, aim to give as wide a variety of foods as possible. This is easier because gluten and non-dairy products can now be given.

INGREDIENTS CHECKLIST

Agar-agar
Bread
Cheese
Chick peas, canned
Cocoa powder
Coconut, flaked
Cottage cheese
Couscous, pasta shapes and rice
Custard
Dried fruit
Eggs
Fresh fruit and vegetables
Frozen spinach
Fruit juice
Herbs and spices
Oats, rolled
Tomato paste
Pear-and-apple spread
Red lentils
Tahini
Tomatoes, canned
Weetabix
Yogurt, plain

	Breakfast	Nap*	Lunch	Dinner	Bedtime
Day 1	Weetabix with banana	Breast or bottle milk	Cheese & Potato Bake Baked apple Juice	Parsnip & Apple Soup Melon Juice	Breast or bottle milk
Day 2	Baby Muesli with grated pear	Breast or bottle milk	Pasta with Napolitana Pasta Sauce Plain yogurt with fruit purée Juice	Broccoli & Cauliflower with Cheese Sauce Papaya Juice	Breast or bottle milk
Day 3	Banana Oatmeal	Breast or bottle milk	Khichri Chocolate Pudding Juice	Ten-minute Tomato Soup Toast strips Plain yogurt with fruit purée Juice	Breast or bottle milk
Day 4	Mashed hard-boiled egg yolk Toast strips Apricot Purée	Breast or bottle milk	Fruity Couscous Fruity Fool Juice	Spinach, Potato & Leek Curry Juicy Gelatin Juice	Breast or bottle milk
Day 5	Weetabix with chopped peaches	Breast or bottle milk	Pasta with Hummus Pasta Sauce Kiwi fruit Juice	Ratatouille Mashed potato Plain yogurt with fruit purée Juice	Breast or bottle milk
Day 6	Baby Muesli with stewed prunes	Breast or bottle milk	Spring Vegetable Risotto Pear Juice	Sandwiches of Grated Cheese with Apple Butter Rice Pudding Juice	Breast or bottle milk
Day 7	Oatmeal with plums	Breast or bottle milk	Lentil Sambhar Mashed banana Juice	Avocado & Cottage Cheese Dip Crudités Plain yogurt with fruit purée	Breast or bottle milk

* *Repeat after lunch and before dinner.*

CHAPTER FOUR

The Independent Spirit

NINE TO TWELVE MONTHS

As your baby approaches his or her first birthday, rate of growth begins to slow down and curiosity and individuality accelerate. As far as feeding is concerned, appetite is no longer the sole contributory factor to mealtime success, if success is equated with introducing the maximum amount of nourishment in the minimum time with the minimum of fuss and mess. There is an old Hindu proverb which Krishnan's father tells me translates roughly as "Your children teach you patience when no one else can." This is just as well, since for the next few years you will need plenty of patience, particularly at mealtimes.

By now, your baby will almost certainly have graduated to a high chair and gained a few teeth and, in keeping with this newly elevated status, will no longer tolerate the ignominy of being forced to eat certain foods by a dominant adult. Having seen the pilot and worked out the screenplay, your baby now wants to be part of the action. Of course, clever parents will let baby think that they are just extras in the big production. The first step toward this is to include some finger foods at every meal (even just a few chunks of steamed vegetable) to give your baby a sense of autonomy.

Now is a good time to invest in suction-based or weighted bowls, spill-proof cups, extra feeding spoons (so you can sneak in mouthfuls while your baby is pushing one piece of pasta around the bowl), and an industrial-sized box of detergent. Make the feeding process less stressful by trying to allow time for your baby to play while eating. This may be easier said than done when you have to get out to work in 10 minutes and your baby is still engrossed in making Weetabix mountains, but, since the child is not going to compromise for some time, you may have to, perhaps by setting the alarm earlier!

The good news is that, for the most part, you will no longer need to prepare special meals (although you will still need to salt your own food separately), freeze food in ice-cube-sized portions, or forgo interesting flavors. You should still moderate fat and sugar intake, peel raw fruit, and avoid whole nuts, raw eggs, and unpasteurized cheeses, but almost anything else goes. Most of the recipes that follow will appeal to adults and older children too—just don't mash or purée their portions. You should now find it possible to select something suitable for your baby to eat from most menus, even if it's only bread and cheese, although when traveling it's wise to take a few sandwiches, some fruit, and a drink.

COMPROMISING SITUATIONS

As conscientious parents, it is all too easy to be seduced into the myth of an ideal eating pattern and try to enforce this upon our children while ignoring the fact that, like us, babies are individuals with rights to preferences, as long as they are not harmful. What really matters is to establish a routine that suits both you and your child. Some babies demand breakfast immediately upon waking and prefer their morning milk before a nap. My son liked milk upon waking and breakfast an hour or so later, and attempts to reverse this pattern proved futile.

Likewise, you should not expect your baby to relish everything you introduce—some flavors are acquired tastes. If your baby rejects a particular dish, try reintroducing it at a later stage. If after several attempts this particular food is still a no-go zone, you can assume that it is disliked, and is not just being rejected for its unfamiliarity. It may also be your baby is a "grazer" rather than one who eats large regular meals; in which case, try to adapt your routine to make time for smaller, more frequent meals.

Your own instincts should tell you when your

baby is being wilful for the sake of it, and when he or she is acting out of genuine desire. Teething, for example, can make some babies very out of sorts and may upset eating patterns. Try offering chilled chunks of fruit to soothe inflamed gums in between meals, and don't be concerned if your baby reverts to a more milk-based diet for a few days when teething.

BALANCING ACT

Older babies still require at least 2½ cups of milk per day. Not all of this need be taken as pure liquid milk—custards, white sauces, and cooked dishes can all contribute to the quota. Most babies enjoy a substantial bottle or breast feeding at bedtime, and this is to be encouraged, for comfort and sustenance, though they shouldn't be left to fall asleep with a bottle. In addition, offer as wide a variety of foods as possible, with plenty of soft, well-cooked fruit and vegetables, some dairy or vegetable protein (such as cheese or legumes), and cereals.

Most pediatricians will offer vitamin drops as dietary supplements, particularly during winter when keeping your baby well wrapped against the weather restricts exposure to daylight, which is vital for the production of vitamin D. By all means, accept these supplements as a precautionary measure, but never regard them as a substitute for a healthy diet.

If you feel that your baby would benefit from vitamin drops, it is a good idea, for vegetarian babies, to opt for the ones which contain iron. As an alternative to vitamin drops, you can give your baby one of the brands of follow-up formula. These contain more of vitamins A, C, and D, plus iron and a good balance of other vitamins and minerals. Follow-up formula is not necessary if you are still using formula milk, which is fine for babies up to twelve months.

SNACKS

At about this age, babies develop an interest in food outside mealtimes. Friends and relatives may well encourage this tendency by offering treats. There is nothing wrong with allowing your baby to eat outside of regular mealtimes, but try to monitor the sorts of foods eaten at these times.

An occasional chocolate or cookie will not do any harm, but tastes developed in early childhood tend to stay into adult life, so it is better to encourage healthier nibbles from the very beginning. Breadsticks, cheese straws, well-rinsed dried fruit, and pieces of fresh fruit or steamed vegetable are all good choices.

PREPARATION

Like most first-time mothers, I was fanatical about sterilizing every piece of feeding equipment throughout the first year. While I still firmly believe that bottles used for milk should be sterilized for as long as your baby uses them (it is almost impossible to clean the inside of a nipple thoroughly and milk is a fertile breeding ground for bacteria), this can seem like a waste of time, as, from the moment your baby is sitting up, every toy, object, and bit of dirt within reach makes straight for the mouth.

Providing you wash your baby's feeding equipment in hot, soapy water and rinse it thoroughly, there is no need to take additional precautions. To minimize the risk of stomach upsets, never save food that has been touched by the spoon your baby is using, and always throw away unfinished milk.

You will notice that most of the following recipes advocate steaming vegetables wherever possible. This is because steaming has been shown to preserve more of the vital nutrients than boiling, as well as being generally less detrimental to texture. Pan-frying food, using a good-quality olive oil, is acceptable (see Falafel, Polenta with Tomato Sauce, Cheese & Peanut Bites), but avoid deep-frying. You can introduce roast vegetables at this age (roast potatoes and parsnips are especially appreciated). When roasting, brush the vegetables lightly with oil (don't sit them in a pool of it) and blot well with paper towels before serving.

Where fresh rather than canned legumes are stipulated (this is relatively rare because I personally believe that life is too short for soaking beans), always boil them rapidly for at least 10 minutes to destroy potentially harmful toxins. When substituting dried beans for canned, use half the stated quantity, since they will roughly double in weight when soaked.

In the recipes, four baby portions are approximately equal to one adult portion, so ten baby portions would serve baby, Mom and Dad. Where a recipe is not freezable, extra portions can be refrigerated then reheated.

TEXTURE

Many of the following recipes may be fed to babies without additional processing. As emphasised in the previous chapter, it is important to introduce texture if you don't wish to end up with a picky toddler who balks at anything bulkier than a chocolate chip. Babies are creatures of habit, so if they are fed mush, then mush is all they will want (although some babies progress more quickly than others to more solid food, and it may depend on whether they are early or late teethers). Make the change gradual. At the beginning of this phase, process food for just a few seconds, introduce grated food alongside purées, and try to contrast textures. Should you be firmly convinced that your baby is congenitally incapable of coping with lumps, offer a chocolate finger cookie and see what happens!

SOUPS, SALADS, AND SNACKS

Apollo Soup

This homely, Italian-style soup is a meal in itself. My son loved it with garlic bread. Once he was old enough to enjoy it unprocessed he insisted we make it using spaceship noodles—hence the very un-Italian title.

MAKES 12 PORTIONS

1 tablespoon olive oil
1 small onion, peeled
and chopped
1 clove garlic, peeled
and finely chopped
6 large ripe tomatoes,
peeled, seeded,
and chopped

2 cups canned cannellini beans,
drained and rinsed
2 cups tiny pasta shapes
1 tablespoon chopped fresh flat-leaf parsley
2 oz cheddar cheese, grated (½ cup)
1 quart vegetable stock
black pepper to taste
a little chopped fresh basil (optional)

Heat the oil and cook the onion until soft. Add the garlic, tomatoes, beans, pasta, parsley, two-thirds of the cheese, and the stock. Season with a little black pepper, if desired. Bring to a boil and simmer for about 30 minutes. Stir in the basil, if using. Leave to cool slightly and purée coarsely in a food processor. To serve, sprinkle with the remaining cheese.

Pumpkin & Apple Soup

I devised this soup on Krishnan's first Halloween as a way of using up the surfeit of pumpkin flesh left from my clumsy attempts at making jack-o'-lanterns. Try serving this with apple chips (at health food stores and some supermarkets) for your baby to dunk.

MAKES 6 PORTIONS

knob of butter
1 teaspoon vegetable oil
scant 1 cup peeled and chopped onion
8 oz pumpkin flesh, finely diced (1 cup)

2 apples, peeled, cored, and chopped
1¼ cups vegetable stock
1¼ cups apple juice

Melt the butter with the oil in a large saucepan. Add the onion and cook for 5–10 minutes or until soft but not brown. Add the pumpkin flesh and apples, stir well, cover, and cook over low heat for 20 minutes, stirring occasionally. Pour in the vegetable stock and apple juice. Bring to a boil and simmer for 30 minutes or until the vegetables are meltingly tender. Let cool slightly, then blend to a smooth consistency.

Sesame Breadsticks

Breadsticks are much healthier for babies to munch on than cookies and they are ideal for appeasing a ravenous infant to whom the phrase "ready in five minutes" means nothing. Because they harden as they cool, they're also very soothing for teething babies. They are easy to make, if a little time-consuming, and they keep well in an airtight container.

MAKES ABOUT 32

1 *envelope quick-rise active dry yeast*
3 *cups white bread flour*
4 *tablespoons butter*
¼ *cup olive oil*

¾ *cup plus 2 tablespoons lukewarm water*
1 *large free-range egg, beaten*
¼ *cup sesame seeds*

Place the yeast and flour in a large bowl and make a well in the middle. Place the butter and oil in a small saucepan and heat until the butter melts. Add the lukewarm water to the butter and oil mixture, then pour this into the well in the flour. Mix into a dough, then turn out onto a floured surface and knead for 10 minutes or until the dough is smooth and elastic.

Divide the dough into 32 pieces and, using the floured palms of your hands, roll into sausage shapes about 8 inches long. Arrange the sticks on greased baking sheets (leaving room for the dough to rise). Brush the sticks with beaten egg, sprinkle with sesame seeds, and bake in an oven heated to 400°F for 20 minutes or until golden. Turn off the heat, leave the door closed and allow the breadsticks to cool and become crisp in the oven.

Cheese Straws

Cheese straws provide another tasty and nutritious nibble, and make a more substantial snack if served with dips. They keep well in an airtight container.

MAKES ABOUT 40

⅔ cup whole-wheat flour
¼ cup mixed nuts,
finely chopped, or ground

4 tablespoons butter
2 oz cheddar cheese, grated (½ cup)
1 large free-range egg, beaten

Sift the flour and stir in the nuts. Cut the butter into the flour. Stir in the cheese, add the egg, and work into a dough. Knead lightly. Roll out on a lightly floured board to approximately ¼ inch. Cut the dough into thin fingers. Bake on oiled baking sheets in an oven heated to 375°F for 12–15 minutes. Cool on a wire rack.

Honey-glazed Corn

Corn is universally loved by babies and older children. This method of cooking gives a lovely sweet result, and your baby will enjoy gnawing at the juicy kernels.

MAKES 3–4 PORTIONS

1 ear corn
1 tablespoon butter

1 teaspoon honey
a little chopped fresh parsley

Cut the corn crosswise into 3 or 4 slices (each piece should be a size that your baby can grasp) and cook in boiling water for 5–10 minutes or until the kernels are tender. Drain and dry. Melt the butter and honey together in a small skillet, then add the corn. Cook gently for about 5 minutes, turning frequently and making sure the honey does not burn. Sprinkle the parsley over the corn and serve.

Cheese & Peanut Bites

Babies love these tasty nibbles with tomato paste or apple purée as a dip. They also make a great portable snack.

MAKES ABOUT 12

3 cups fresh white bread crumbs
4 oz cheddar cheese, grated (1 cup)
1 small onion, chopped
1 small carrot, chopped

1 tablespoon chopped parsley
1 tablespoon smooth peanut butter
2 free-range eggs, separated

Place 2 cups bread crumbs in the bowl of a food processor with the cheese, onion, carrot, and parsley, and process until fine. Add the peanut butter and egg yolks and process again until the mixture holds together. Divide the mixture into 12 pieces and roll them into balls. Dip each ball in egg white, then coat in the remaining bread crumbs. Place the coated balls on an oiled baking sheet and bake in an oven heated to 375°F for about 20 minutes, turning them after 10 minutes, until crisp and golden. Serve warm or cold.

Minty Yogurt Dip

As well as being good with Falafel, this mild, refreshing dip is delicious with sticks of raw carrot or cucumber. Krishnan used to adore it with fingers of warm naan bread.

MAKES 5 PORTIONS

1-inch piece of cucumber
⅔ cup plain yogurt
1 teaspoon finely chopped fresh mint

Peel, grate, and drain the cucumber (in a colander). Combine the yogurt, cucumber, and finely chopped mint, and leave for at least 30 minutes to let the flavors develop fully.

☺ | ☹

Falafel

These mildly spicy Middle Eastern croquettes make excellent finger food for babies. If you are apprehensive about giving your baby exotic flavors you can omit the spices altogether—the falafel will still taste good.

MAKES 12

15-oz can chick peas (garbanzo beans), drained and rinsed
1 small onion, finely chopped
1 small red pepper, seeded, finely chopped, and steamed until tender
1 clove garlic, peeled and finely chopped

1 tablespoon chopped fresh flat-leaf parsley
¼ teaspoon ground cumin
¼ teaspoon ground coriander
1 free-range egg, beaten
a little flour for coating
1 tablespoon vegetable oil

Place the first seven ingredients in the bowl of a food processor and work to a coarse purée. Add the egg and blend again briefly to combine. Divide the mixture into 12 portions and, using the palms of your hands, shape into little "link sausages." Roll each lightly in flour and chill for 30 minutes.

Heat the oil in a skillet and cook the falafel gently over medium heat for about 10 minutes, turning frequently, until golden. Serve with tomato paste or Minty Yogurt Dip.

☺ | ☹ | . | ❄

Apple, Beet & Carrot Salad

It's a good idea to introduce babies to salads as soon as larger quantities of raw vegetables are acceptable; otherwise unfamiliarity will breed contempt. Just as adults aren't enthralled by a lettuce leaf and a slice of cucumber, babies too like colorful and interesting combinations.

MAKES 4 PORTIONS

1 carrot, rinsed, peeled, and finely grated
⅓ cup finely grated cooked beet
½ apple, peeled, cored, and finely chopped
1 tablespoon raisins, rinsed

½ tablespoon olive oil
½ teaspoon cider vinegar
pinch of sugar
1 oz cheddar cheese, grated (¼ cup)

Place the carrot, beet, apple, and raisins in a bowl and stir to combine. Mix together the olive oil and cider vinegar and season with a little sugar. Pour this dressing over the vegetables and fruit—toss to combine. Serve with grated cheese.

Muffin Pizzas

While your baby is still consuming diminutive portions, it seems hardly worth making fresh pizza dough in such tiny quantities. For a speedy treat, store-bought English muffins make an acceptable pizza crust and this simple topping is easy to prepare.

MAKES 4 PORTIONS

2 English muffins
8-oz can crushed tomatoes
1 tablespoon olive oil

3 oz mozzarella cheese, grated (¾ cup)
1 teaspoon chopped fresh oregano

Split the muffins. Place the tomatoes in a small skillet, add the oil, bring to a boil, and simmer for 15 minutes, stirring occasionally, until thick. Drain off any excess liquid, strain the tomato sauce to remove the seeds, then purée and leave to cool. Spoon equal amounts of the tomato sauce onto the muffin halves, place the cheese on the tomato, and sprinkle the oregano on top. Bake in an oven preheated to 450°F for 10–12 minutes, or until the pizzas are golden brown and bubbling.

Rice Salad

Don't be tempted to use leftover rice for this appealing salad unless the rice is still warm—heat is needed to develop the flavors. Pepper, corn, and peas are always popular with babies, but you can also include green beans, mushrooms, or fava beans. For added sweetness, a little fresh pineapple or orange also works well.

MAKES 10 PORTIONS

¾ cup basmati rice, rinsed, and soaked in cold water for 20 minutes
½ small red pepper, seeded, finely chopped, and steamed until tender
⅓ cup each frozen peas and corn, cooked

3 tablespoons dried currants
2 tablespoons olive oil
1 tablespoon orange juice
½ clove garlic, crushed
a little chopped fresh flat-leaf parsley

Cook the rice until tender, then drain. Stir well using a fork and let cool slightly. Stir in the cooked vegetables and currants. Mix together the oil, orange juice, and garlic, then pour this dressing over the rice mixture and stir to combine. Leave to cool completely. Before serving, sprinkle the parsley over the salad and stir again.

Avocado & Orange Salad

Avocados are a valuable source of vitamins, and most babies seem to enjoy their creamy texture. Choose a very sweet variety of orange or, for variety, substitute a sweet pear for the orange.

MAKES 4 PORTIONS

1 *very ripe avocado*
1 *orange*

Peel and pit the avocado, then cut the flesh into small chunks. Using a sharp knife, cut the top and base off the orange, then peel away the skin. Carefully make incisions between the pith and the orange so you are left with skinless segments. Reserve any juice. Chop the orange segments in half and combine with the avocado. Add the orange juice and toss again. Serve at once with fingers of whole-grain bread.

PASTA SAUCES

Busy parents will probably identify with my belief that you can never have too many pasta sauces in your repertoire. The four that follow are all good with any pasta shape. Now that your baby is older, offer some of the many excellent stuffed fresh pastas—Krishnan especially liked mushroom and cheese, and spinach and ricotta. A suitable pasta portion is 1–2 oz dried pasta.

Spinach & Ricotta Pasta Sauce

MAKES 8 PORTIONS

2 tablespoons butter
10 oz frozen chopped leaf spinach, defrosted
a little grated nutmeg

½ cup ricotta cheese
1 oz pecorino cheese, grated (⅓ cup)

Melt the butter and, when it is bubbling, add the spinach. Cook until the spinach is heated through, stirring often. Season with the grated nutmeg. Stir in the cheeses and heat gently without boiling. Serve with pasta shapes.

☺ ☹

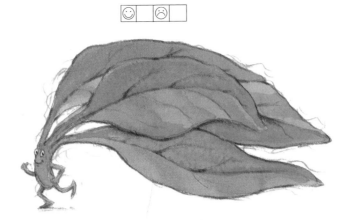

Three-pepper Pasta Sauce

MAKES 6 PORTIONS

2 tablespoons olive oil
1 clove garlic, finely chopped
1 medium red pepper, seeded and
finely sliced
1 medium green pepper, seeded and
finely sliced

1 medium yellow pepper, seeded and
finely sliced
1 onion, peeled and thinly sliced
½ teaspoon dried oregano
a little chopped fresh basil
2 large tomatoes, peeled, seeded,
and chopped

Heat the oil and add the garlic, peppers, onion, and herbs. Cover and cook over very low heat for about 20 minutes or until the vegetables are very tender. Add the chopped tomatoes, raise the heat, and let the mixture bubble for 5 minutes. Remove from the heat and purée in a food processor. Reheat to serve.

Broccoli with Béchamel

MAKES 4 PORTIONS

8 oz broccoli flowerets
2 tablespoons butter
3 tablespoons all-purpose flour
1¼ cups milk

1 bay leaf
1 slice onion
2 sprigs parsley, stems left on
a little grated nutmeg

Cut the broccoli flowerets into bite-size pieces and steam for about 5 minutes, until tender but not wilted. Set aside. Melt the butter, stir in the flour, and simmer for about 3 minutes. Add the milk, whisking until the sauce bubbles and is thick and smooth. Add the bay leaf, onion, and parsley, lower the heat, and simmer for 15–20 minutes, stirring occasionally and adding extra milk if the sauce thickens too much. Remove the onion, bay leaf, and parsley. Season the sauce with a little grated nutmeg and stir in the cooked broccoli.

Mushroom & Four-cheese Pasta Sauce

MAKES 4 PORTIONS

1 tablespoon butter
½ onion, peeled and finely chopped
1 clove garlic, peeled and finely chopped
1½ cups wiped and quartered mushrooms

1 oz each Bel Paese, cheddar, Gruyère and
pecorino cheese, grated (¼ cup each)
⅔ cup light cream

Melt the butter and gently cook the onion and garlic until soft but not brown. Add the mushrooms and cook for 5 minutes longer. Remove from the heat. Stir in the cheeses and cream, and stir until melted (you may need to return the pan to the heat to achieve this, but do not let the sauce boil).

MAIN COURSES

Lentil Hot Pot

In our house this dish is irreverently known as "bottom of the refrigerator stew," because it invariably appears when I have put off going shopping and am left with a few kitchen staples. Despite the frugal ingredients, it tastes quite sumptuous.

MAKES 10 PORTIONS

1 tablespoon vegetable oil
1 onion, peeled and chopped
1 clove garlic, crushed
1 large potato, peeled and cubed
2 carrots, peeled and diced
2 celery ribs, rinsed and chopped

1¼ cups red lentils, picked over and rinsed
14-oz can crushed tomatoes
2 teaspoons tomato paste
1 bay leaf
½ teaspoon dried oregano
2½ cups vegetable stock

Heat the oil and cook the onion and garlic until soft but not brown. Add the potatoes, carrots, celery, and lentils, and stir to coat the vegetables with the oil. Add the tomatoes, tomato paste, herbs, and the vegetable stock. Bring to a boil, cover, and simmer for 40–45 minutes, or until the lentils and vegetables are very tender. Remove the bay leaf. Before serving, mash baby's portion of lentils and vegetables using a fork.

☺ ☹ ❄

Vegetable Crumble

Babies seem to love both sweet and savory crumbles. This simple recipe lends itself to all sorts of vegetable permutations. Here I have used root vegetables and squash, but zucchini, cauliflower, and peppers make tasty and colorful alternatives.

MAKES 10 PORTIONS

1 tablespoon vegetable oil	2 oz orange cheddar cheese, grated (½ cup)
1 onion, peeled and chopped	pinch of grated nutmeg
1 clove garlic, peeled and finely chopped	TOPPING
1½ cups peeled and cubed parsnip	3 tablespoons butter, softened
1½ cups peeled and cubed rutabaga	½ cup whole-wheat flour
1½ cups peeled and cubed butternut squash	½ cup rolled oats
2 tablespoons butter	1 tablespoon mixed chopped fresh parsley and
2 tablespoons all-purpose flour	chives (optional)
1½ cups milk	¼ cup walnuts, toasted and ground

Heat the oil and gently cook the onion and garlic until soft but not brown. Meanwhile, steam the prepared vegetables for about 10 minutes or until tender. Set the vegetables in a colander for a few minutes to allow any excess liquid to evaporate.

Melt the butter in a saucepan. Add the flour and cook, stirring, for 2 minutes. Gradually incorporate the milk to form a smooth sauce, then simmer gently for 2 minutes. Remove the sauce from the heat and stir in the cheese and nutmeg. Add the cooked onions and vegetables to the sauce, mix thoroughly and transfer to an oiled baking dish.

To make the crumble topping, rub the softened butter into the flour and oats, and stir in the herbs (if using) and nuts. Spoon the crumble over the vegetables and smooth the top. Bake in an oven preheated to 400°F for about 35 minutes or until the topping is golden and the filling bubbling. Mash baby's portion coarsely with a fork and serve with lightly steamed green beans or broccoli.

Vegetarian Shepherd's Pie

The texture of bulgur is ideal for a shepherd's pie and adds extra nutrition to this tasty vegetarian version of a British mainstay.

MAKES 6–8 PORTIONS

⅓ cup bulgur
3 cups peeled and cubed potatoes
a little butter and milk, for mashing
2 tablespoons vegetable oil
1 onion, finely chopped
1 clove garlic, peeled and finely chopped
2½ cups wiped and
quartered mushrooms

2 medium zucchini, wiped,
trimmed, and diced
1 carrot, peeled and diced
2 tablespoons chopped fresh parsley
8-oz can crushed tomatoes
2 tablespoons tomato paste
¾ cup vegetable stock
4 oz cheddar cheese, grated (1 cup)

Place the bulgur in a bowl, cover with boiling water, and leave to stand for 15 minutes or until the grains absorb the liquid. Stir well with a fork to fluff. Boil the potatoes for about 15 minutes or until tender, then drain and mash with a little butter and milk.

Heat the oil, add the onion and garlic, and cook until soft but not brown. Add the mushrooms, zucchini, and carrot, and continue cooking for 2 minutes. Stir in the parsley, tomatoes, tomato paste, and stock. Bring to a boil, cover, and simmer until the vegetables are tender, about 15 minutes.

Add the soaked bulgur to the vegetables, stir, and continue cooking for 5 minutes. Transfer the mixture to a shallow baking dish and spread the mashed potato evenly on top, roughing up the surface with a fork. Sprinkle the cheese over the top. Bake in an oven preheated to 400°F for 30 minutes, or until golden. Serve with vegetarian gravy (available from health food stores).

Barley Pot

When I was a child, barley broth was a regular wintertime supper, and I remember loving the creamy texture of the shiny pearl-like grains of barley. Although it has been replaced by designer pastas as an ingredient in soups and stews, I think barley is still worth using. Krishnan used to love this served with garlic bread.

MAKES 3 PORTIONS

2 teaspoons vegetable oil
½ clove garlic, peeled and finely chopped
½ onion, peeled and chopped
1 small carrot, peeled and diced
2 celery ribs, rinsed and finely sliced
1 teaspoon mild paprika
1¼ cups vegetable stock

8-oz can crushed tomatoes
1 generous tablespoon pearl barley, rinsed
1 leek, rinsed, trimmed, and finely sliced
1 parsnip, peeled and cubed
6 oz cauliflower flowerets
½ teaspoon chopped fresh
rosemary (optional)

Heat the oil and cook the garlic, onion, carrot, and celery for 5 minutes. Stir in the paprika and cook for a minute longer. Add the remaining ingredients and simmer for 40 minutes or until the vegetables are tender. Mash baby's portion coarsely before serving.

Potato Hash

This is a slightly more grown-up version of Krishnan's beloved Cheese & Potato Bake (see page 52). Baby peas and corn make good accompaniments.

MAKES 4 PORTIONS

12 oz new potatoes
1 tablespoon butter
½ onion, peeled and finely chopped
1 beefsteak tomato, peeled,

seeded, and chopped
⅓ cup light cream
2 oz cheddar cheese, grated (½ cup)
2–3 tablespoons whole-wheat bread crumbs

Scrub the potatoes and boil them in their skins. When they are tender, drain, cube, and spread them over the bottom of a small, shallow gratin dish. Melt the butter over very low heat and gently cook the onion until soft but not brown. Add the tomato and continue cooking for 5 minutes or until the tomato is tender. Stir in the cream and cheese, and stir constantly until the cheese almost melts. Pour the sauce over the potatoes. Sprinkle the bread crumbs on top, and brown under a preheated broiler.

Lentil Moussaka

It is one of the many small milestones of babyhood when you can actually look forward to sharing food with your baby. This was one of the first dishes that Krishnan and I enjoyed together. Le Puy lentils are small French lentils which have a superior flavor and texture to other varieties, but other lentils could be substituted.

MAKES ENOUGH FOR MOM, DAD, AND BABY, OR 6 PORTIONS

1¼ cups Le Puy lentils
1 large eggplant, wiped and trimmed
1 tablespoon olive oil, plus a little extra for brushing
1 small onion, peeled and finely sliced
1 small red pepper, seeded and thinly sliced
1 clove garlic, peeled and crushed

1 teaspoon Italian seasoning
1 cup drained and finely chopped sun-dried tomatoes
1½ cups pure strained tomatoes, such as Pomi
2 oz cheddar cheese, grated (½ cup)
½ cup whole-wheat bread crumbs

Rinse the lentils thoroughly. Place them in a saucepan, cover with cold water, and bring to a boil. Boil rapidly for 10 minutes, then reduce the heat and simmer for 30–40 minutes or until tender. Drain well.

Slice the eggplant into rounds and place on a broiler pan. Brush lightly with olive oil, broil until golden, then turn over and repeat the process. Set the cooked eggplant aside.

Heat the oil and cook the onion and pepper until soft. Stir in the garlic and seasoning, and turn off the heat. Place half the lentils in the bottom of a baking dish, top with half the eggplant, half the onion and pepper mixture, and half of both the sun-dried tomatoes and strained tomatoes. Repeat the layers. Mix together the cheese and bread crumbs and sprinkle them over the top. Bake in an oven preheated to 350°F for about 30 minutes, or until golden and bubbling. Purée baby's portion coarsely before serving.

☺ ☹ ❄

Hungarian Stuffed Zucchini

I have always found overgrown, stuffable summer squashes bland, but babies seem to love them—and, prepared in this way, they are both tasty and nutritious.

MAKES 4 PORTIONS

½ very large zucchini, cut lengthwise
generous ½ cup peeled and sliced carrots
generous ½ cup peeled and chopped parsnips
approximately ⅓ cup vegetable stock
1 tablespoon butter
1 small onion, chopped

½ red pepper, seeded and diced
¾ cup wiped and quartered mushrooms
8-oz can crushed tomatoes
⅓ cup frozen corn, defrosted
⅔ cup plain yogurt
2 tablespoons mild paprika

Remove the seedy center of the zucchini. Boil the squash, still intact, for about 10 minutes, until soft (you will need a fish kettle or a large, deep stock pot). Drain the zucchini, reserving the liquid. Boil the carrots and parsnips in this liquid until tender. Drain the carrots and parsnips (again reserving the liquid) and mash them together. Add enough vegetable stock to the reserved liquid to make ⅔ cup and set aside.

Melt the butter and gently cook the onion until soft but not brown. Add the pepper and continue cooking for 10 minutes. Add the mashed carrot and parsnip to the pepper mixture, along with the mushrooms, and cook for 2 minutes longer. Stir in the tomatoes, corn, and stock mixture. Bring to a boil then simmer for 25 minutes.

Mix together the yogurt and paprika. Add this to the vegetable mixture and stir well. Pile this mixture into the shell of the cooked zucchini, wrap in foil, and bake in an oven preheated to 350°F for 45 minutes, or until the zucchini is very tender. Cut the stuffed zucchini into quarters and mash baby's portion. Serve with cooked rice and yogurt.

Butter Bean & Leek Gratin

Next to the perennially popular baked beans, butter beans are my son's favorite legume. They seem to have a natural affinity for the sweet pungency of leeks, which makes this dish a great success.

MAKES 10–12 PORTIONS

*3 medium leeks, trimmed, rinsed, and
finely chopped*
½ small cauliflower, divided into flowerets
2 tablespoons butter
1 small onion, finely chopped
1 clove garlic, peeled and finely chopped

1 tablespoon all-purpose flour
1 teaspoon ground coriander
1 cup mixed vegetable stock and milk
14-oz can butter beans, drained and rinsed
50 g/2 oz cheddar cheese, grated (½ cup)
1-oz package unsalted potato chips, crushed

Steam the leeks and cauliflower for about 10 minutes or until tender; set aside. Melt the butter and gently cook the onion and garlic until soft but not brown. Sprinkle the flour onto the onion and continue cooking, stirring, for 3 minutes. Add the coriander, then stir in the stock and milk to make a smooth sauce (you may need to add a little more liquid to achieve a smooth consistency). Simmer the sauce gently for a couple of minutes.

Stir the beans, leeks, and cauliflower into the sauce. Transfer to a baking dish. Mix together the cheese and chips and sprinkle them over the top of the vegetables. Bake in an oven preheated to 350°F for 30 minutes, until golden and bubbling. Mash with a fork or purée coarsely. Serve with steamed green vegetables.

Zucchini, Cauliflower & Chick Pea Curry

This mild and creamy recipe contains the merest hint of spice and no chili, so it is safe to give to your baby.

MAKES 12–15 PORTIONS

1 tablespoon vegetable oil

1 small onion, finely chopped

1 tablespoon all-purpose flour

1–2 teaspoons mild curry paste

1 tablespoon tomato paste

2 tablespoons smooth peanut butter

2½ cups vegetable stock

½ medium cauliflower, divided into flowerets

4 medium zucchini, cubed

15-oz can chick peas (garbanzo beans), drained and rinsed

1¼ cups plain yogurt

Heat the oil and cook the onion until soft but not brown. Sprinkle the flour over the onion and cook, stirring, for 2–3 minutes. Add the curry paste, tomato paste, and peanut butter, then gradually stir in the stock. Simmer for 5–10 minutes.

Meanwhile, steam the cauliflower and zucchini until tender, about 5–12 minutes (add the zucchini after the cauliflower, since it will take less time). Add the cauliflower, zucchini, and chick peas (garbanzo beans) to the sauce, cover, and simmer gently for 20–30 minutes. Turn off the heat and let the curry stand for 10 minutes. Stir in the yogurt. Mash or purée. Serve with rice and banana slices.

Chinese Fried Rice

If your baby enjoys pronounced flavors, you could add a little grated ginger and garlic to this dish (cooked with the onion and carrot). Do make sure that the egg is thoroughly cooked before adding the rice. You could also add a few toasted sesame seeds before serving. Soy sauce is high in sodium, so it should be used with caution—this recipe contains just a dash.

MAKES 8 PORTIONS

1 tablespoon vegetable oil
3 scallions, trimmed and sliced
1 medium carrot, peeled and diced
½ green pepper, seeded and diced
⅓ cup frozen peas, defrosted
1½ oz beansprouts, rinsed

1 large tomato, peeled, seeded, and chopped
1 free-range egg, beaten
1 cup cooked basmati rice
1 teaspoon light sesame oil
dash of soy sauce (optional)

Heat the oil in a large skillet or wok, add the scallions and carrot, and stir-fry for a couple of minutes. Add the pepper, peas, beansprouts, and tomato, and stir-fry for 2 minutes longer. Push the vegetables to one side of the pan, pour in the beaten egg and cook, stirring continuously, until it is well scrambled. Add the rice, mix well, and stir-fry until it is heated through. Drizzle the sesame oil and soy sauce over the rice, and serve.

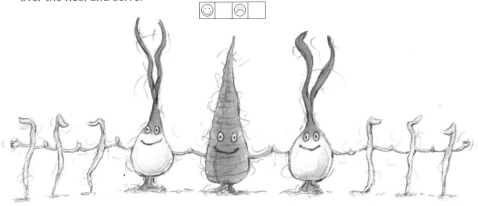

Polenta with Tomato Sauce

Polenta is a northern Italian staple made from cornmeal. Because it has rather a bland flavor and soft texture, it is ideal for babies. Serve it with the sweet tomato sauce recipe given below, or any of the pasta sauce recipes (the sauce will freeze).

MAKES 8 PORTIONS

1 quart water
2 cups polenta
4 tablespoons butter
SAUCE
1 tablespoon olive oil
1 onion, finely chopped

1 clove garlic, peeled and finely chopped
2 red peppers, seeded and finely chopped
14-oz can tomatoes
1 tablespoon tomato paste
1 free-range egg, beaten
extra cornmeal for coating

Bring the water to a boil, gradually sprinkle the polenta onto the water and stir well until smooth. Add the butter, cover, and cook for about 20 minutes, stirring frequently until thick and creamy. Pour the cooked polenta into an oiled dish about 13 x 9 inches and leave to cool and set.

To make the sauce, heat the oil and cook the onion and garlic until soft but not brown. Add the peppers and continue cooking for 5 minutes. Add the tomatoes and tomato paste, bring to a boil, and simmer for 20 minutes or until the sauce is reduced. Cut the cold polenta into squares. Coat with beaten egg and cornmeal and pan-fry until golden brown. Drain well on paper towels. To serve, pour the sauce over the polenta.

SWEETS AND DESSERTS

Apple & Raisin Muffins

These delectable, low-fat cakes are perfect for breakfast or an afternoon snack, and can even be served with custard or ice cream for a more substantial dessert.

MAKES 12

1¼ cups milk
¾ cup oat bran
2 large free-range eggs
5 tablespoons butter, melted
3 tablespoons turbinado sugar
½ teaspoon vanilla extract

⅓ cup whole-wheat flour
⅔ cup all-purpose flour
2 teaspoons baking powder
1 apple, peeled, cored, and chopped
¼ cup raisins, soaked in orange juice for a
few hours

Grease 12 muffin pan cups. Place the milk and oat bran in a bowl. Beat together the eggs, melted butter, sugar, and vanilla extract. Add the egg mixture to the oat and milk mixture.

Sift the flours and baking powder together and stir in the chopped apple. Combine the two mixtures, add the soaked, drained raisins, and stir thoroughly. Spoon the mixture into the prepared pan. Bake in an oven preheated to 375°F for 25–30 minutes or until golden and risen. Remove from the pan at once.

Oat Cookies

Oats are a valuable source of vitamins and fiber, so these wholesome, sugar-free cookies are an ideal, enjoyable treat.

MAKES 24

⅔ cup whole-wheat flour
1 cup rolled oats
1 stick butter, softened

¼ cup apple butter
1 large free-range egg, beaten

Place the flour and oats in a bowl and cut in the butter. Mix in the apple butter (you may need to soften this first by warming it over a pan of hot water or in a microwave oven). Add the egg, and mix into a firm dough.

Roll out the dough on a lightly floured surface to about ¼ inch thick, then stamp out into shapes using cookie cutters. Place on greased cookie sheets and bake in an oven preheated to 375°F for 10–15 minutes or until golden. Let cool slightly on the cookie sheets before transferring to a wire rack to cool completely. Store in an airtight container.

☺ ☹

Strawberry Crunch

My son very appropriately once described this as "upside-down crisp." If you don't want to use cream, thick custard sauce is every bit as good.

MAKES 8 PORTIONS

6 tablespoons butter
2 oz flaked coconut
¾ cup rolled oats
⅓ cup whole-wheat flour

1¼ cups whipped cream
⅔ cup plain yogurt
1 pint strawberries, rinsed and hulled
a little toasted coconut to decorate

Place the butter, coconut, oats, and flour in a food processor and work until the butter is cut in. Grease a shallow baking pan and press the mixture in to a depth of 1 inch. Bake in an oven preheated to 375°F for about 20 minutes or until golden. Leave the crunch to cool in the pan on a wire rack. Cut it into sections and then crumble these to cover the bottom of a shallow serving dish. Whisk together the cream and yogurt and spread this over the crunch base. Top with chopped strawberries and chill for at least one hour so the base becomes soft. To serve, decorate with toasted coconut.

☺ ☹

Carrot Cake

Older babies enjoy cake as an occasional treat, but plain sponge cakes can be a little dry for them to cope with. Carrots make this cake very moist and therefore easy for babies to eat.

MAKES 8–10 PORTIONS

1⅔ cups whole-wheat flour
1 teaspoon ground cinnamon
½ teaspoon grated nutmeg
½ tablespoon baking powder
1 stick butter

⅓ cup honey
½ cup raw cane sugar,
such as turbinado
2 cups peeled and
finely grated carrots

Sift together the flour, spices, and baking powder. Melt the butter, honey, and sugar together over low heat, then add to the flour mixture, stirring to combine. Stir in the grated carrots. Place the batter in a well-greased 8 x 4-inch bread pan and bake in an oven preheated to 325°F for 60–80 minutes or until a skewer inserted into the middle comes out clean. Cool on a wire rack. Store in an airtight container.

☺ ☹ ❄

Blueberry & Peach Cobbler

Blueberries and peaches make the most delectable combination imaginable,
second only to Krishnan's favorite, blueberry and strawberry.

MAKES 8 PORTIONS

1 *lb ripe peaches*
2 *tablespoons granulated sugar*
pinch of grated nutmeg
pinch of ground cinnamon
½ *teaspoon lemon juice*
1 *pint blueberries, rinsed and dried*

TOPPING
⅓ *cup all-purpose flour*
½ *teaspoon baking powder*
2 *tablespoons butter*
½ *tablespoon granulated sugar*
½ *beaten free-range egg*
1½ *tablespoons milk*

Peel the peaches (score the skins into four, then plunge them into boiling water to make this easier), pit them, and slice thinly. Place the prepared peaches in a pan over low heat and cook gently until the juices begin to bubble. Remove from the heat, leave to cool, and drain the peaches, reserving the juice. Stir the sugar, spices, and lemon juice into the reserved juice. Place the poached peach slices and the blueberries with the spiced juice in a baking dish.

To make the topping, sift together the flour and baking powder, then cut in the butter. Stir in the sugar. Mix the egg and milk together and stir into the flour mixture to form a dough. Roll out the dough on a floured board and cut into small rounds. Place the rounds on top of the fruit and brush with milk. Bake in an oven preheated to 400°F for 20 minutes or until golden brown. Serve with plain yogurt or custard.

Mixed Fruit Compote

This is delicious served with yogurt for breakfast, or as a dessert with custard or ice cream. It will keep for 3 to 4 days in the refrigerator.

MAKES 8 PORTIONS

1 oz dried pears
1 oz pitted dried prunes
3½ oz dried peaches
3½ oz dried apple rings
1 oz dried banana chips

1 oz golden raisins
1½ cups orange juice
3 cloves
1-inch piece cinnamon stick
1 teaspoon grated orange peel

Place all the ingredients in a pan with ½ cup water. Bring to a boil, cover, and simmer until all the fruits are very tender. Remove the cloves and cinnamon, and leave to cool. Chill until serving time.

Baked Egg Custard

Egg custard is another classic dish that is perennially popular with babies. I have used apricot spread in this recipe, but strawberry spread is equally good.

MAKES 4 PORTIONS

2 teaspoons granulated sugar
2 large free-range eggs

1¼ cups milk
2 tablespoons sugar-free apricot spread

Beat the sugar and eggs together until the sugar dissolves and the mixture is frothy. Whisk in the milk and apricot spread. Strain the mixture into a buttered 2½-cup baking dish. Bake (in a bain-marie if preferred) in an oven preheated to 300°F for 30 minutes or until set. Leave to cool. Chill until serving time.

Mango, Kiwi & Papaya Fruit Salad

Exotic fruits are naturally high in fructose, vitamins, and minerals, so they are a valuable addition to your baby's diet.

MAKES 8 PORTIONS

juice of 1 large orange
1 very ripe mango, peeled, pitted, and chopped

2 kiwi fruit, peeled, sliced, and quartered
1 ripe papaya, peeled, seeded, and chopped

Pour the orange juice over the prepared mango, kiwi fruit, and papaya. Serve with yogurt or ice cream. ☺ ☹

Homemade Yogurt

Yogurt is an invaluable baby food, on its own and in other dishes. Making your own is cheap and easy, as well as being a good way of using up a surfeit of milk, if, like me, you are never organized enough to keep on hand exactly the right amount of milk. The yogurt used as a starter must be live.

MAKES ABOUT 2½ CUPS

2¼ cups whole milk
1 tablespoon formula powder or

non-fat dry milk
1 tablespoon live yogurt

Mix the milk with the powder and heat until almost boiling. Let cool until luke-warm. Whisk in the yogurt and pour the mixture into a sterilized, wide-necked vacuum bottle. Leave for 6–8 hours. Transfer to a nonmetallic container, cover, and refrigerate for 6 hours. Use within a week.

NINE TO TWELVE MONTHS MENU CHART

This Menu Chart shows how you might integrate some of the recipes in this chapter into a balanced diet, which can be adapted for the rest of the family.

INGREDIENTS CHECKLIST

Apple butter
Apricot spread
Breads and muffins
Breakfast cereals
Bulgur, pasta shapes, pearl barley, polenta, and rice
Butter beans and cannellini beans, canned
Cheese
Chick peas (garbanzo beans), canned
Coconut, flaked
Cream
Custard sauce
Dried fruit
Eggs
Fresh fruit and vegetables
Frozen vegetables
Fruit juices
Herbs and spices
Honey
Mixed nuts
Oat bran
Oats, rolled
Peanut butter
Lentils, Le Puy and red
Sesame seeds
Sun-dried tomatoes
Tomatoes, canned
Tomatoes, pure, strained
Tomato paste
Unsalted potato chips
Yeast
Yogurt, plain

* *Milk with breakfast and before mid-morning nap each day.*
** *Juice with lunch, afternoon snack, and dinner.*

		Breakfast*	Lunch**	Afternoon snack	Dinner	Bedtime
Day 1		Weetabix Banana Milk	Pasta with Three-pepper Pasta Sauce Plain yogurt with fruit purée	Pumpkin & Apple Soup Sesame Breadsticks Oat Cookies	Vegetable Crumble Mixed Fruit Compote Custard	Milk
Day 2		Oatmeal with chopped apple	Vegetarian Shepherd's Pie Baked Egg Custard Fruit	Honey-glazed Corn Avocado & Orange Salad Plain yogurt with fruit purée	Pasta with Mushroom & Four-cheese Pasta Sauce Mango, Kiwi & Papaya Fruit Salad	Milk
Day 3		Scrambled egg Toast fingers Pear	Butter Bean & Leek Gratin Green vegetables Fruit	Sandwiches Plain yogurt with fruit purée	Potato Hash Carrot Cake	Milk
Day 4		Weetabix Strawberries Plain yogurt with fruit purée	Lentil Moussaka Apple, Beet & Carrot Salad Rice Pudding	Falafel with Minty Yogurt Dip Fruit	Hungarian Stuffed Zucchini Fruit	Milk
Day 5		French Toast Apple Purée	Zucchini, Cauliflower & Chick Pea Curry Rice Plain yogurt with fruit purée	Muffin Pizzas Baked Egg Custard	Pasta with Spinach & Ricotta Pasta Sauce Fruit	Milk
Day 6		Mixed Fruit Compote Yogurt Toast	Lentil Hot Pot Vegetables Fruit	Apollo Soup Cheese Straws Plain yogurt with fruit purée	Cheese & Peanut Bites Apple Purée Rice Salad Blueberry & Peach Cobbler	Milk
Day 7		Cornflakes Apple Toasted raisin bread	Pasta with Broccoli with Béchamel Strawberry Crunch	Polenta with Tomato Sauce Apple & Raisin Muffins	Barley Pot Fruit	Milk

CHAPTER FIVE

The Growing Gourmet

TODDLERS

From first birthday until starting school, your toddler will gain in independence and ability at an amazing rate. No longer a baby, he or she is now a determined participant in every aspect of daily life, and that includes meals. For parents, this stage can be tremendous fun, but it can also be frustrating when it comes to trying to ensure a balanced diet is eaten. Food is no longer just fuel but an object of fascination to be explored, experimented with, and only occasionally eaten. The important thing is to remain relaxed and keep everything in perspective as your lovingly prepared, nutritionally sound dinner ends up in your child's hair or on the carpet. Toddlers are quick to sense parental anxiety and even quicker to learn how to use this to manipulate parents to their own ends. Coax, cajole, and encourage toddlers to eat, but never force them; otherwise the kitchen table will rapidly come to resemble a combat zone.

All children go through phases of finicky eating, picking at food, or sometimes not eating at all. However worrisome these phases may be, bear in mind there are few recorded instances of toddlers who have succeeded in starving themselves to death before their fifth birthday. If children are of normal weight and height, then you can rest assured they are consuming a few calories along with the fresh air you naively imagine sustains them. Toddlers have small tummies and even smaller attention spans, which means it is physically difficult for them to eat enough at one meal to keep them going through until the next, and almost impossible for them to concentrate on the job once the initial hunger pangs have been satisfied. By all means work at introducing them to the concept of three meals a day, but don't expect them to get it for a good few years, and be prepared for a certain amount of between-meals grazing.

HEALTHY EATING HABITS

What toddlers eat, rather than when and how much, is what really matters. Experts now agree that eating habits and food preferences learned in childhood play a significant role in preventing the degenerative diseases that plague us in later life. Although vegetarians have a head start in meeting the dietary targets established by the World Health Organization, I have met more than one vegetarian child whose diet consists almost entirely of fries, cola, chips, and pizza. One mother, whose three-year-old was a regular dinner visitor, apologetically warned me her son would eat only pasta shapes and french fries. As Dr. Christopher Green, author of the excellent *Toddler Taming* (Vermilion) drily comments on such restricted diets: "Is this mother telling me that junior gets up in the morning, takes the keys of the Volvo, drives down to the supermarket, loads up a trolley with chips and chocolate, drives home and eats them?"

Broadly speaking, you should try to make sure your toddler eats plenty of fruit and vegetables, full-fat dairy products (small people actually need, rather than crave, those extra calories), and complex carbohydrates (bread and cereals). Try to restrict the intake of sweetened and refined foods such as cakes and cookies, and keep salt to a minimum. However, don't be overzealous in enforcing these ground rules—the occasional chocolate bar or french fry is an indulgence, not a poison. Nor on any account should you attempt to feed your toddler a high-fiber, low-fat diet. This could lead to what doctors now disparagingly diagnose as "Muesli-Belt Syndrome," a form of malnutrition experienced by a number of children whose parents force-feed them high-fiber "hamster food," including large amounts of unrefined foods such as whole-grain bread, brown rice, and whole-wheat pasta, in the erroneous belief it is good for them. Toddlers need filling up with nutrients, not sawdust.

FOOD AS FUN

For toddlers, just as much as for adults, food should be a pleasure, not a chore. Variety is the key to stimulating a sense of enjoyment around food and mealtimes. If you feed your child a monotonous diet, eating will become a bore and your toddler will grow increasingly suspicious of new and unfamiliar foods. Small children can be amazingly adventurous in their tastes, if they are given the opportunity. From the age of one, the only dietary restriction that applies is the avoidance of whole nuts because of the very real risk of choking. Otherwise, the supermarket is your toddler's oyster.

Like adults, toddlers eat first with their eyes, so food should look appealing and be attractively presented. There is no need to go to the extremes of carving tomato roses or radish fans, but a bowl of gray-looking mush is not going to do much to stimulate a reluctant appetite, whereas bright colors, interesting shapes, and different textures will. A fruit salad, for example, will have far more toddler appeal if the fruits are prepared individually and arranged in a pattern on a plate than if they are presented as a bowl of homogenous lumps. A simple salad of grated carrot and apple will entrance with its contrasting colors. Keep portions small so as not to overwhelm. You can always add more if the first portion disappears quickly.

From a very early age, most children are fascinated by food preparation. When time, patience, and safety considerations permit, allow your child to help. My son's idea of a perfect Sunday morning is to be allowed to stand on a chair next to me, popping pea pods or spreading tomato sauce on pizza crusts. For a special treat, we make chocolate Rice Krispie cakes for him to take to preschool on Monday. The pride with which he bears those misshapen mountains to his classmates makes all the mess worthwhile. Handling food helps him to feel involved—even if this consists simply of selecting the pasta shapes which he wants to accompany his sauce.

Up until their first birthday, most children are quite happy to allow parents to feed them, but increasing independence inevitably leads to insistence on doing it themselves. Grit your teeth, protect your carpets, keep a damp cloth handy, and resist the temptation to intervene too much. It's worth investing in a set of special flatware with chunky, toddler-friendly handles to aid the process. At first it will be slow and messy, but, as your child's dexterity increases, more of the food will eventually reach its intended destination and satisfaction and confidence will be gained from having managed alone.

Shared family meals are an ideal which is not always possible or practical, given the demands of modern life. On those occasions when it is necessary for your toddler to eat independently, try to avoid the temptation to plonk him or her in front of the electronic babysitter (TV). Instead, make an occasion of the affair by preparing a picnic to be shared with inanimate friends in the yard, or make a play tent with a clothes drying rack and an old blanket for pretend camping. My son especially enjoys snacking "at sea," pretending he is afloat in his old baby bath.

A TIME FOR TOGETHERNESS

As parents, in our eagerness to ensure that our toddlers consume enough of the right foods to maintain healthy growth, it is easy to lose sight of the fact that food performs a key role in the bonding process. Providing wholesome, home-cooked food is in itself an expression of our care for those we love. Mealtimes should be a social event; they are often the only times when the family can sit down together and exchange news and ideas in a relaxed, unhurried atmosphere. Even before children are able to join in conversation, they can learn to appreciate this special time together. And never underestimate the power of food as education. Much of my son's knowledge of different countries and ways of life has been inspired by discussions stemming from the food on his plate. Also, children who regularly eat with adults tend to have fewer problems grasping the rudiments of table manners—example is better than instruction. Also, most children really enjoy eating out, with its sense of occasion. Italian and Chinese restaurants are good first choices, because the waiters often have a relaxed attitude toward small people and will make a great fuss over diminutive customers.

By the age of two or so, many toddlers will be attending a playgroup or preschool and developing a social life of their own. Encourage this by inviting little friends for lunchtime play sessions and giving the food a party feel (there are lots of suggestions for suitable menus at the end of this chapter). Children who learn at an early age to relate to their peers and to share find it much easier to cope when the time comes to start school.

ABOUT THE RECIPES

The recipes in this chapter are designed to introduce your toddler to as wide a variety of tastes and textures as possible while still appealing to the rest of the family. In the early days you may find you need to be a little cautious with the flavorings and seasonings, but by the time your toddler is three or four there should be no reason to modify the recipes, provided you yourself do not have an embarrassing sodium habit or a penchant for fiery curries. By introducing your toddler to delicious, wholesome food at an early age you are making one of the greatest investments possible in your child's future health and happiness. *Bon appetit!*

SOUPS, SANDWICHES & SNACKS

Four Seasons Soup

This colorful, nutritious soup is an ideal way of introducing toddlers to vegetable chunks. Let them use pieces of crusty bread to fish out the different vegetables, and see how many they recognize.

MAKES 4 ADULT PORTIONS

1 tablespoon olive oil
1 onion, finely chopped
1 parsnip, peeled and chopped
1½ cups peeled and diced rutabaga
1½ cups peeled and diced potato
1 teaspoon Italian seasoning (optional)

2 tablespoons tomato paste
2½ cups light vegetable stock
1 zucchini, diced
½ cup frozen peas
salt and black pepper to taste

Heat the oil, add the onion, parsnip, rutabaga, and potato, and cook gently, without browning, for 5 minutes. Add the Italian seasoning (if using), tomato paste, and stock. Bring to a boil, then cover and simmer for 25 minutes. Add the diced zucchini and peas. Season, cover, and simmer for 5–10 minutes longer.

Beet & Apple Soup

Toddlers love colorful food, so the deep, rich hue of this sweet and satisfying soup is highly appealing. My son calls it "lipstick soup" because of the slight stain it leaves around the mouths of messy eaters!

MAKES 4 ADULT PORTIONS

1 tablespoon olive oil
2 medium raw beets, peeled and diced
1 apple, peeled, cored, and chopped
1 medium potato, peeled and grated

2 cups light vegetable stock
⅔ cup apple juice
salt and black pepper to taste
¼ cup plain yogurt

Heat the oil, add the beets and apple, and cook gently for 3–4 minutes. Add the potato and stock. Bring to a boil, then cover and simmer for 30 minutes or until the beets are tender. Cool slightly, then add the apple juice and purée in a blender until smooth. Reheat, season to taste, and serve with a swirl of plain yogurt.

Carrot & Orange Soup

This became a favorite with my son on a skiing vacation in France, during which the vegetarians in the party received carrot soup and an omelette at every meal. Nowadays, we have it less frequently, served with fingers of warmed pita bread or crunchy garlic croutons.

MAKES 4 ADULT PORTIONS

1 tablespoon olive oil
1 onion, finely chopped
5 cups rinsed and diced carrots
grated peel and juice of 1 orange

2 cups light vegetable stock
⅔ cup milk
salt and black pepper to taste

Heat the oil, add the onion and carrots, cover and cook gently for 5–10 minutes. Add the orange peel and juice, and the stock, and bring to a boil. Simmer for 20 minutes or until the carrots are tender. Cool slightly, then add the milk. Purée in a blender. Reheat and season to taste.

Sandwiches

Sandwiches make terrific toddler food since they can often be enjoyed without parental intervention. They also offer great scope for ingenuity. Try using different breads (though anything with seeds should be avoided), making pinwheels or shapes using cookie cutters, or even using light and dark bread to make striped sandwiches. Reluctant eaters can usually be coaxed by the prospect of a picnic, even if it is in the living room, so, for trouble-free dinners, it's worth investing in a lunch box featuring your child's favorite cartoon character. I have found the following fillings to be particularly successful .

CREAM CHEESE & HONEY FACES

MAKES 4 MINI SANDWICHES

2 *slices whole-wheat bread, lightly buttered*
2 *tablespoons cream cheese*
1 *tablespoon honey*
handful of raisins

Spread the bread with the cheese and honey, and sandwich together. Remove the crusts and stamp out four small rounds using a cocktail pastry cutter. Stud with raisins to make eyes, noses, and mouths.

PEANUT BUTTER & BANANA FINGERS

MAKES 3 FINGERS

1 *slice each white and whole-grain bread, buttered*
1 *tablespoon smooth peanut butter*
1 *small banana, mashed*

Spread the white bread with the peanut butter, and top with mashed banana. Cover with the brown bread. Cut off the crusts and cut into three fingers.

CARROT & HUMMUS POCKETS

MAKES 2 MINI PITAS

2 *mini pita breads*
3 *tablespoons Hummus (see page 40)*
1 *small carrot, grated*

Warm the pita breads and split lengthwise. Mix together the hummus and grated carrot and use the mixture to fill the pita bread.

BRIE & BLACK GRAPE

MAKES 4

2 *oz ripe Brie cheese, sliced*
2 *slices fruited quick bread, lightly buttered*
4 *black grapes, halved and seeded*

Arrange the Brie on one slice of the bread. Top with the grape halves and cover with the remaining slice of bread. Cut off the crusts and cut into quarters.

ITALIAN FLAG ROLLS

MAKES 4 ROLLS

1 *small avocado, peeled, pitted, and mashed*
2 *tomatoes, thinly sliced*
4 *soft white mini rolls, split and buttered*
salt and black pepper to taste
4 *slices mozzarella cheese*

Divide the avocado and tomato between the rolls and season lightly. Top with a slice of mozzarella cheese.

CREAM CHEESE & BEAN SLICES

MAKES 4

2 *tablespoons garlic-and-herb-flavored cream cheese*
2 *tablespoons canned red kidney beans,*
drained and rinsed
4 *slices French bread*

Mash together the cream cheese and kidney beans. Spread evenly over the slices of French bread.

Baked Potatoes

Baked potatoes are another great toddler food, but the key to their acceptance is to get the potato fluffy and light and the skin deliciously crunchy. Sadly, speedy though they may be, microwave ovens cannot achieve this. You need to boil the potatoes for 20 minutes before transferring them to a hot oven (400°F) for 20–30 minutes, depending on size. Split the potatoes, scoop out the flesh, mash the flesh with a little butter, pile it back into the skins, and fill the potatoes with any of the following suggestions.

CREAM CHEESE & CHIVES

FOR 2 POTATOES

4 *oz cream cheese and chives (½ cup)*
1 *tablespoon chopped mushrooms*

Mix together the cheese and mushrooms and spoon into two prepared potatoes.

BEEFLESS SPAGHETTI SAUCE

See the recipe for Beefless Spaghetti Sauce on page 113. The leftover sauce is ideal as a potato filling. Sprinkle grated pecorino cheese over the top before serving.

CREAMY MUSHROOMS

FOR 2 POTATOES

2 tablespoons butter
1½ cups wiped and sliced mushrooms
1 tablespoon all-purpose flour
1¼ cups milk
salt and black pepper to taste
grated nutmeg to taste

Melt the butter and cook the mushrooms until soft. Sprinkle the flour onto the mushrooms and cook, stirring, for 1–2 minutes. Stir in the milk gradually. Bring to a boil, simmer for 1 minute, and add seasoning and nutmeg to taste. Spoon the creamy mushrooms into two prepared potatoes, and serve with green salad.

BEANFEAST

FOR 2 POTATOES

7-oz can baked beans
2 oz cheddar cheese, grated (½ cup)
black pepper
dash of vegetarian Worcestershire sauce

Heat the beans and stir in the cheese. Season with pepper and Worcestershire sauce. Spoon into two prepared potatoes.

GREEN & GOLD

FOR 2 POTATOES

⅓ cup frozen peas
⅓ cup frozen corn
½ cup cottage cheese
salt and black pepper to taste

Cook the peas and corn according to the directions on the packages. Drain the cooked vegetables and mix them with the cottage cheese. Season to taste and spoon into two prepared potatoes.

RATATOUILLE

See the recipe for Ratatouille on page 53, and use to fill prepared potatoes.

Cheese & Herb Scones

These scones are super with soup for lunch or with dinner,
but my son especially likes them for breakfast.

MAKES 24 MINI SCONES

1¾ cups whole-wheat flour
4 teaspoons baking powder
pinch of salt
1 teaspoon dry mustard powder
1 teaspoon Italian seasoning

3 tablespoons butter
4 oz cheddar cheese, grated (1 cup)
⅔ cup milk, plus a little extra for brushing
top of scones before baking

Sift together the flour, baking powder, salt, mustard, and herbs. Cut in the butter. Stir in half the cheese and work into a soft dough with the milk. Turn the mixture onto a lightly floured board and knead gently. Roll out to a thickness of approximately 1 inch and cut into circles. Sprinkle the remaining cheese over the tops. Bake on an oiled baking sheet in an oven preheated to 425°F for 10 minutes, or until the scones sound hollow when tapped underneath. Cool on a wire rack.

Muffin Rabbits

To toddlers, rarebit and rabbit are easily confused words, and I have never had the heart to explain the difference to my son. Hence, I always serve this supper staple cut into "ears," that is, halves.

MAKES 4

1 English muffin, split
a little Marmite or Vegemite
1 tablespoon butter

2 scallions, finely chopped
2 oz cheddar cheese, grated (½ cup)
a little milk

Toast the muffin lightly and spread thinly with Marmite or Vegemite. Melt the butter, add the scallions and cook gently until soft. Stir in the cheese, adding a little milk to give a smooth consistency and, when the mixture is creamy, spread it on the muffin. Cut the muffin into halves and serve with ketchup.

Potato Cakes

These are wonderful for both breakfast and dinner, served either German-style, with applesauce, or more conventionally with broiled tomatoes and mushrooms.

MAKES 8

2¼ cups mashed potatoes
⅔ cup all-purpose flour
1 stick butter, melted

salt and black pepper to taste
chopped fresh parsley to taste
extra butter for cooking

ash together the potatoes and flour. Work in the melted butter, seasonings, and parsley. Shape the dough into little cakes approximately 1½ inches in diameter. Melt a little butter in a large skillet.. When the butter is sizzling, add the potato cakes and cook for 5–7 minutes on both sides, or until golden brown. Serve immediately.

☺ ☹ ❄

Frittata

Most toddlers adore omelettes, which makes them the ideal vehicle for introducing different vegetables. Krishnan calls this Italian-style omelette "breakfast supper" because of its similarity to scrambled eggs.

MAKES 4 ADULT PORTIONS

1 tablespoon olive oil
4 zucchini, sliced
1 red pepper, seeded and chopped
1 potato, peeled, boiled, and diced
1 clove garlic, peeled and finely chopped
1 bunch of scallions, finely chopped

1 tablespoon chopped fresh basil
1 tablespoon chopped fresh parsley
salt and black pepper to taste
6 free-range eggs, beaten

eat the oil in a large skillet, add the zucchini and pepper, and cook gently until soft. Stir in the potato and garlic. Add the scallions, herbs, and seasonings to the eggs. Pour the egg mixture over the vegetables in the skillet. Cook gently until golden underneath. Place the pan under a preheated broiler until the top of the frittata is brown. Serve, hot or cold, cut into wedges.

☺ ☹

Pasta Salad

A lot of toddlers, my own included, are unenthusiastic about salads, but if you include their preferred ingredients, like pasta, they won't even notice they are eating salad.

MAKES 4 ADULT PORTIONS

1¾ cups (dry weight) pasta shapes, cooked
1 red pepper, peeled, seeded, and blanched
1 green pepper, peeled, seeded, and blanched
⅔ cup canned corn kernels

⅔ cup peas, cooked
2 tomatoes, peeled, seeded, and chopped
3 tablespoons olive oil
salt and black pepper to taste

Mix together the pasta and all the prepared vegetables in a bowl. Add the olive oil, season to taste, and toss lightly.

Three-color Salad

This scaled-down version of the classic *insalata tricolore* has the bright colors, mild flavors, and creamy textures which appeal to most children.

MAKES 4 ADULT PORTIONS

1 pint cherry tomatoes, quartered
1 medium avocado, peeled, pitted, and chopped

1¼ cups cubed mozzarella cheese
2 tablespoons olive oil
salt and black pepper to taste

Mix together the tomatoes, avocado, and cheese. Pour the olive oil over the salad, season to taste, and serve with crunchy bread.

Curried Rice Salad

This slightly spicy, sweet, and nutritious salad is an excellent accompaniment to grilled or broiled tofu kebabs or burgers.

MAKES 6 ADULT PORTIONS

1 *generous cup basmati rice, rinsed and soaked in cold water for 20 minutes*
1 *teaspoon turmeric*
salt
15-*oz can green or brown lentils, drained*
⅔ *cup peas, cooked*

4 *oz baby spinach, rinsed, stems removed, and finely sliced*
DRESSING
¼ *cup olive oil*
1 *tablespoon soy sauce*
1 *tablespoon mango chutney*
½ *teaspoon mild curry powder*

Cook the basmati rice in boiling water until tender, adding the turmeric and salt to taste. Drain well. Stir in the lentils, peas, and spinach. Mix together the dressing ingredients. Pour the dressing over the salad and toss. Chill.

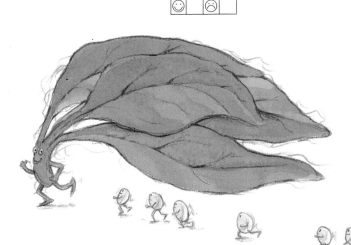

Garlic Bread

Any preconceptions you may have about toddlers not liking garlic will disappear when you confront them with a plate of garlic bread. For a more nutritious snack, add a little grated cheese to the butter mixture.

FOR 1 BAGUETTE

1 *small baguette (French bread)*
6 *tablespoons butter, softened*
1 *teaspoon chopped fresh parsley*

2 *cloves garlic, peeled and very finely chopped*
salt and black pepper to taste

Slice the baguette, but do not cut completely through. Mix the butter, parsley, and garlic together, then season to taste. Spread the mixture onto the cut surfaces of the bread, wrap the baguette in foil, and place in a hot oven at 400°F for 10–15 minutes or until the butter melts and the crust crisps.

MAIN COURSES

Beefless Spaghetti Sauce

I've yet to come across a child who isn't enthusiastic about this tasty sauce, whether it is served with pasta, or in shepherd's pie, or as a filling for baked potatoes. The quantity is generous because it makes an excellent freezer standby.

MAKES 8 ADULT PORTIONS

¼ cup olive oil
1 large onion, chopped
2 cloves garlic, peeled and crushed
1 tablespoon chopped fresh basil
scant 1 teaspoon dried oregano
1 bay leaf
1 carrot, peeled and diced
1 rib celery, finely chopped
1 red pepper, seeded and chopped

2½ cups quartered mushrooms
2 tablespoons tomato paste
⅔ cup red wine
1 tablespoon dark soy sauce
salt and black pepper to taste
8-oz can crushed tomatoes
2 x 15-oz cans green or brown lentils, drained
1 tablespoon chopped fresh flat-leaf parsley

Heat the oil, add the onion, garlic, basil, oregano, and bay leaf, and cook until the onions are transparent. Add the carrot, celery, and red pepper, cook for a few minutes longer, then add the mushrooms. When the mushrooms begin to wilt, stir in the remaining ingredients. Bring to a boil, cover, and simmer for approximately 40 minutes. Leave to cool, transfer to a food processor, and blend coarsely (if you prefer a chunkier texture, blend only half the mixture). Before serving, reheat and adjust seasoning.

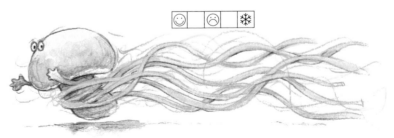

Spinach & Mushroom Lasagne

A preschool nature session on the subject of mushrooms left my son highly suspicious of all varieties of mushroom for some time. Such was his passion for this richly satisfying lasagne, however, that he conveniently overlooked their inclusion.

MAKES 6 ADULT PORTIONS

MUSHROOM SAUCE
2 tablespoons butter
2 onions, peeled and chopped
3½ cups wiped and thinly sliced mushrooms
2 cloves garlic, peeled and crushed
1 tablespoon chopped fresh flat-leaf parsley
1 tablespoon chopped fresh basil
¼ cup tomato paste
14-oz can crushed tomatoes (replace some juice with red wine for a richer sauce)
1 tablespoon soy sauce
1 teaspoon honey
salt and black pepper to taste

CHEESE SAUCE
3 tablespoons butter
¼ cup all-purpose flour
2½ cups milk
8 oz cheddar cheese, grated (2 cups)
pinch of dry mustard powder
pinch of grated nutmeg

8 oz spinach lasagne (the type requiring no precooking)
1 lb chopped frozen spinach, defrosted and drained

For the mushroom sauce, melt the butter and cook the onions until transparent. Add the mushrooms, garlic, and herbs and continue cooking. Then stir in the tomato paste, tomatoes, soy sauce, and honey. Season and simmer for 10 minutes.

Prepare the cheese sauce: melt the butter, add the flour, and cook, stirring, for 2–3 minutes. Gradually incorporate the milk. Let the sauce bubble for 1 minute, then turn off the heat and stir in half the grated cheese and the seasonings.

Grease a large baking dish and layer the lasagne, cheese sauce, spinach, and mushroom sauce, finishing with a layer of lasagne topped with cheese sauce. Sprinkle the remaining cheese on the top and bake in an oven preheated to 350°F for 40 minutes. Let stand for 10 minutes before serving.

Tomato & Mascarpone Pasta Sauce

This creamy sauce goes well with any pasta. Let toddlers choose the pasta shapes—such as wheels, corkscrews, and alphabets—and you have a nutritious meal that's also fun to eat.

MAKES 4 ADULT PORTIONS

2 tablespoons olive oil
1 onion, finely chopped
1 clove garlic, peeled and finely chopped
1 tablespoon chopped fresh flat-leaf parsley
1 tablespoon chopped fresh basil leaves

14-oz can crushed tomatoes
½ teaspoon honey
salt and black pepper to taste
8 oz mascarpone cheese (1 cup)

Heat the oil and cook the onion and garlic until very soft but not brown. Stir in the herbs and cook for 1 minute, then add the tomatoes, honey, and seasonings. Add 6 tablespoons water, bring to a boil, and let the sauce bubble gently for 30 minutes. Stir in the mascarpone, heat through, and adjust seasoning.

Treasure Island Couscous

When my son was still rather reluctant about lumps in food we used to pretend that the couscous in this recipe was the beach and that the vegetables were the treasure buried in the sand. The subterfuge worked beautifully.

MAKES 6 ADULT PORTIONS

*2 tablespoons olive oil, plus a little for
the couscous
1 large onion, peeled and chopped
1 cup sliced carrot
1 cup peeled and cubed rutabaga
1 clove garlic, peeled and finely chopped
½ teaspoon grated gingerroot
pinch of ground cinnamon
½ cup chopped dried apricots
⅓ cup raisins*

*1 quart light vegetable stock
15-oz can chick peas, drained and rinsed
1 cup wiped and sliced okra
1 zucchini, sliced
2 cups couscous
4 tablespoons butter
salt and black pepper to taste
1–2 tablespoons chopped fresh cilantro
leaves (optional)*

Heat the oil, add the onion, carrot, and rutabaga and cook for 10 minutes. Add the garlic, gingerroot, and cinnamon and cook for 2 minutes. Stir in the apricots and raisins, pour in the stock, and simmer until the carrots are tender and the dried fruits plump, approximately 20 minutes. Add the chick peas, okra, and zucchini and continue cooking for 10–15 minutes longer.

Meanwhile, prepare the couscous by placing 1½ cups of water in a pan. Add 1 teaspoon of salt and a little oil, and bring to a boil. Remove from the heat, stir in the couscous and leave for 3 minutes, or until the couscous has absorbed the water. Stir in the butter and fluff up the grains using a fork.

Season the vegetables, sprinkle the cilantro (if using) over them, and serve on a bed of couscous.

Cauliflower & Potato Bake

This more substantial version of cauliflower with cheese sauce has a crunchy crisp topping to maximize its toddler-tempting power.

MAKES 6 ADULT PORTIONS

1 large cauliflower
3 tablespoons butter
3 cups cooked and sliced waxy new potatoes
4 oz Gruyère cheese, grated (1 cup)
salt and black pepper to taste

2 free-range eggs, beaten
2 tablespoons each plain yogurt and light cream, mixed
1½ oz reduced-fat potato chips, finely crushed

Break the cauliflower into flowerets, then steam them until just tender. Generously butter a gratin dish and layer the cauliflower, potatoes, and grated cheese, lightly seasoning each layer with salt and pepper. Finish with a layer of cheese. Mix together the beaten eggs and yogurt. Spoon this over the cheese and sprinkle the crushed chips on the top. Bake in an oven preheated to 400°F for 30 minutes or until golden brown and bubbling.

Frosty Stew

My son calls this hearty, homely dish "Frosty Stew" because it appears only on bitterly cold days. For younger toddlers, lightly mash the vegetable chunks. Serve it with creamy mashed potatoes or herbed dumplings, perfect for keeping out the cold.

MAKES 4 ADULT PORTIONS

¼ cup vegetable oil
12 oz pearl onions, peeled
1 clove garlic, peeled and crushed
2 ribs celery, sliced
2 large carrots, peeled and cut into chunks
2 large parsnips, peeled and cut into chunks
1½ cups peeled and cubed pumpkin flesh
1 tablespoon all-purpose flour

1¼ cups vegetable stock
generous 1 cup stout, such as Guinness
1 tablespoon vegetarian Worcestershire sauce
2 tablespoons chopped fresh flat-leaf parsley
2 bay leaves
1 bouquet garni
2 tablespoons tomato paste
salt and black pepper to taste

Heat the oil in a large flameproof casserole and cook the onions, garlic, and celery until golden. Add the remaining vegetables and continue cooking until they are light brown. Sprinkle the flour over the vegetables and stir well to incorporate. Add the stock, stout, Worcestershire sauce, herbs, and tomato paste. Season to taste and bring to a boil, stirring. Cover and cook in an oven preheated to 350°F for about 45 minutes or until all the vegetables are tender.

Bread & Cheese Pudding

A main-course version of the nursery favorite, Bread Pudding (see page 130), this is delicious with a salad of sweet cherry tomatoes.

MAKES 4 ADULT PORTIONS

2 tablespoons butter, plus a little for spreading
1 large leek, very finely chopped
½ teaspoon dried thyme
4 oz sharp cheddar cheese, grated (1 cup)
3 oz Parmesan cheese, grated (¾ cup)

½ teaspoon dry mustard
1 tablespoon chopped fresh chives (optional)
8 medium slices white bread, crusts removed
3 free-range eggs
2 cups milk
salt and black pepper to taste

Melt the butter in a skillet, add the leek and thyme, and cook slowly for approximately 20 minutes, until soft and golden. Mix together the cheeses, mustard, and chives. Lightly butter the bread and a large baking dish. Place four slices of the bread in a single layer in the bottom of the dish, spread with the leek mixture, and sprinkle half the cheese over the top. Place the remaining bread and cheese on top. Beat together the eggs and milk and season lightly. Pour this mixture over the bread and cheese. Leave to stand for 30 minutes, then bake at 375°F for 30 minutes or until golden and risen.

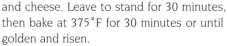

Wild West Beans

All children love baked beans, so the commercial brands (especially the low-salt and -sugar varieties) are an excellent standby. However, it is fun to make your own version when time permits.

MAKES 6–8 ADULT PORTIONS

1 tablespoon olive oil
½ onion, peeled and finely chopped
1 clove garlic, peeled and crushed
8-oz can crushed tomatoes
2 tablespoons soy sauce
⅔ cup apple juice

2 tablespoons molasses
dash of vegetarian Worcestershire sauce
1 tablespoon Dijon mustard
2 x 15-oz cans Great Northern or navy
beans, drained
salt and black pepper to taste

Heat the oil in a saucepan, add the onion and garlic, and cook until soft. Stir in the tomatoes, soy sauce, apple juice, molasses, Worcestershire sauce, and mustard. Bring to a boil, then simmer for 10–15 minutes or until the liquid is slightly reduced. Add the drained beans and simmer for 20–30 minutes. Season and serve with Mini Cheese Sausages (see page 135), baked potatoes, vegetarian hot dogs or homemade Mini Veggie Burgers (see page 136).

☺ ☹ ❄

Vegetarian Sausage &
Apple Casserole

Like most children, my son loves sweet-and-sour taste combinations, so this wholesome casserole devised by my friend Heather Mairs, Director of The Vegetarian Society Cookery School in England, is a real hit. Any of the excellent brands of vegetarian sausage now on the market can be used. For a special treat, serve this piled into popovers or split biscuits.

MAKES 4–6 ADULT PORTIONS

1 *package vegetarian sausages (about 8)*
1½ *lb waxy potatoes, peeled*
and cubed
2 *tablespoons vegetable oil*
1 *large onion, peeled and finely chopped*
2 *cloves garlic, peeled and crushed*
1 *bay leaf*

2 *teaspoons dried thyme*
3 *cups sliced carrots*
1 *large apple, peeled, cored, and cubed*
14-*oz can crushed tomatoes*
1¼ *cups apple juice or cider*
1 *tablespoon tomato paste*
salt and black pepper to taste

Broil the sausages until brown, then chop them into chunks and set aside. Boil the potatoes in salted water for 5 minutes and drain. Heat the oil, cook the onion gently until soft, then add the garlic and herbs and continue cooking for 2 minutes. Add the carrots and apple and cook for 5 minutes longer. Stir in the tomatoes, apple juice or cider, and tomato paste. Bring to a boil and simmer for 15 minutes. Finally add the potatoes and sausages to the tomato mixture, season, and simmer for 10–15 minutes.

| ☺ | ☹ | ❄ |

Prehistoric Potato Hash

My father, a Lancashire lad and committed carnivore, believed a child deprived of "tater hash" was a child denied one of life's great pleasures. To convince him his nonmeat-eating grandson was not going to grow up underprivileged, I devised this vegetarian version for them both to enjoy. Though ridiculously simple, it works.

MAKES 4–6 ADULT PORTIONS

1 lb reconstituted TVP chunks (textured vegetable protein)—follow directions on package
1 large onion, peeled and chopped
1 large carrot, peeled and diced
1½ lb floury potatoes, peeled and cubed

salt and black pepper to taste
vegetable stock
8 oz piecrust dough, defrosted if frozen
1 free-range egg, beaten

Place the TVP, along with the prepared vegetables, in a deep baking dish, season and pour on enough stock to cover. Cover and cook in an oven preheated to 350°F for approximately 1½–2 hours. Remove from the oven and raise the oven temperature to 400°F. Roll out the dough to form a lid for the dish, using the trimmings to make dinosaur shapes to decorate. Glaze with the beaten egg and return to the oven for 15–20 minutes or until golden brown. Serve with steamed cabbage.

Stir-fried Vegetables

Even children who are particularly picky about vegetables seem to love them stir-fried. Vary the combinations according to what is in season and your child's preferences. I find that baby corn, broccoli, mushrooms, zucchini, and peppers all work well. Also, this is one of the few ways that lettuce becomes acceptable to many small children.

MAKES 6 ADULT PORTIONS

MARINADE
2 tablespoons soy sauce
grated peel and juice of 1 orange
1 clove garlic, peeled and crushed
1 tablespoon honey

1½ cups cubed tofu
2 tablespoons vegetable oil
few drops light sesame oil

2 cloves garlic, peeled and finely chopped
1 bunch scallions, finely sliced
2 lb prepared mixed vegetables: carrots,
red and green peppers, broccoli, baby
corn, zucchini, lettuce
1 cup almond halves or cashew nuts
1 tablespoon soy sauce
1 tablespoon mirin (Chinese rice
wine) or sherry

Mix together the soy sauce, orange peel and juice, garlic, and honey, and stir in the cubed tofu. Let marinate for at least 1 hour. Heat the oils in a wok or large skillet. Stir-fry the marinated tofu for 2–3 minutes, then remove from the oil and drain on paper towels.

Stir-fry the garlic and scallions in the wok for 1–2 minutes. Add the vegetables according to the length of time they need to cook: carrots and peppers first, then broccoli, corn, zucchini, and lettuce last. Stir-fry until cooked through but still crisp.

Meanwhile, finely chop or grind the nuts, then toast them in a separate dry pan until golden. Add the soy sauce, mirin or sherry, and tofu to the vegetables and stir briskly. Scatter the nuts over the vegetables. Serve with boiled rice.

Paella

Although the list of ingredients does seem rather daunting, this paella is extremely easy to prepare and ranks among my son's "best-ever dinners." Omit the olives if your toddler hasn't yet acquired the taste—in our house they always disappear first.

MAKES 8 ADULT PORTIONS

2 tablespoons olive oil
1 onion, peeled and chopped
2 cloves garlic, peeled and chopped
1 red pepper, seeded and chopped
1 green pepper, seeded and chopped
1 bay leaf
1 beefsteak tomato, peeled, seeded,
and chopped
4 tablespoons butter
2 cups arborio rice
1 quart light vegetable stock mixed with

white wine
½ teaspoon paprika
1 teaspoon turmeric
salt and black pepper to taste
1 package vegetarian hot dogs
1 cup frozen peas
1 cup frozen corn
1½ cups mushrooms
½ cup ripe olives (optional)
chopped fresh flat-leaf parsley and lemon
wedges to serve

Heat the oil in a wok, add the onion, garlic, peppers, and bay leaf, and cook for 5 minutes. Stir in the tomato, then the butter, and, when bubbling, the rice, stirring until it is thoroughly coated with butter.

In another pan, heat the stock and wine, adding the paprika, turmeric, and seasonings. When the rice is opaque, pour the liquid onto it, stir well, and bring to a boil. Reduce the heat, cover tightly, and simmer for 20 minutes without removing the lid. Meanwhile, cook the sausages according to the directions on the package, then cut them into chunks. Add the sausages and all remaining ingredients to the rice, cover and cook for 10–15 minutes longer. To serve, scatter chopped parsley on top and garnish with lemon wedges.

Vegetable Curry

The creamy sweetness of the coconut milk makes this curry appeal to even the most timid of palates, especially when accompanied by Indian pappadums ("big chips, Mommy"), slices of banana, and plain yogurt.

MAKES 4 ADULT PORTIONS

1 tablespoon vegetable oil
1 onion, peeled and finely chopped
1 clove garlic, peeled and chopped
1 tablespoon mild curry powder
2 lb prepared vegetables: carrots,

potatoes, cauliflower, and green beans
1¼ cups canned coconut milk
salt and black pepper to taste
1 cup frozen peas
⅔ cup plain yogurt

Heat the oil, add the onion and garlic, and cook until soft. Stir in the curry powder and cook for 1–2 minutes. Add the prepared vegetables and cook for a few minutes, stirring to coat them with the spices. Pour in the coconut milk (add a little extra water if necessary), cover, and simmer gently until all the vegetables are almost tender, about 20 minutes. Season, add the frozen peas, and cook for 15 minutes longer. Stir in the yogurt, heat through, and serve on a bed of boiled rice.
Note: If this is to be frozen, add yogurt after defrosting.

Leek Tart

Caramelized leeks give this quiche-like tart a slight sweetness which all children love. Salad makes a good accompaniment.

MAKES 6 ADULT PORTIONS

8 oz piecrust dough, defrosted if frozen
4 tablespoons butter
3 cups trimmed, rinsed, and
finely chopped leeks
2 tablespoons all-purpose flour

1¼ cups milk
3 oz cheddar cheese, grated (¾ cup)
2 free-range eggs, beaten
salt and black pepper to taste
grated nutmeg to taste

Roll out the dough and use to line an oiled 9-inch tart pan. Melt half the butter in a pan, add the leeks, cover, and cook for 20 minutes, until soft and golden. Meanwhile, in another pan, melt the remaining butter, stir in the flour, and cook, without allowing it to brown, for 1–2 minutes. Heat the milk, then gradually beat it into the flour mixture until a smooth sauce forms. Simmer for 1–2 minutes. Stir the leeks, cheese, beaten egg, seasonings, and nutmeg into the sauce. Pour the mixture into the crust and bake in an oven preheated to 375°F for 30–35 minutes, until golden brown and risen.

SWEET TREATS

Thomas' Lemon Tart

My son's godmother, Anne Lawman, used to make this quick, cheesecake-like dessert for her own grandson, and now it's a solid favorite with my son, too. If the mixture does not thicken, add a little more lemon juice.

MAKES 8–10 ADULT PORTIONS

4 *tablespoons butter*
2 *tablespoons turbinado sugar*
4 *oz graham crackers, crushed*
1¼ *cups heavy cream*

14-oz can condensed milk
grated peel and juice of 2 large lemons
green grapes to decorate

Melt the butter, add the sugar, and stir in the cracker crumbs. Press the mixture into the bottom and sides of an 8-inch tart pan. Place the cream, condensed milk, lemon peel and juice in a large bowl and beat until well blended and slightly thickened. Pour the mixture into the crust and chill until set, at least 3 hours, before decorating with grapes.

Chocolate Baked Bananas

My son, in common with most small children, is passionately fond of both bananas and chocolate. This unusual recipe makes a little chocolate go a long way, which keeps us both happy.

MAKES 4 ADULT PORTIONS

4 large bananas, unpeeled
4 oz semisweet chocolate, chopped

4 teaspoons mixed nuts, finely chopped, or ground

Trim the ends of the bananas, but do not peel. Wipe the skins and split the bananas lengthwise, but not through the skin underneath. Press the chopped chocolate into the split of each banana, then wrap them tightly (individually) in foil. Bake in an oven preheated to 400°F for 25 minutes or until the banana skins are blackened and the flesh soft. Sprinkle the chopped nuts over the chocolate filling and serve. Your toddler will enjoy scooping the delicious sticky mixture directly out of the skin.

Raspberry Trifle

Fresh raspberries can be a little tart for toddlers' tastes, but the gelatin and cake offset this. For a change, make this in individual glass sundae dishes, or with strawberries and strawberry gelatin.

MAKES 6 ADULT PORTIONS

1 raspberry-jam-filled jelly roll
1 pint raspberries, rinsed and hulled
1 package vegetarian raspberry gelatin crystals (at health food stores)

1¼ cups thick custard
1¼ cups heavy cream (or a mixture of cream and plain yogurt), whipped
1 oz milk chocolate, shaved

lice the jelly roll and use it to line a deep, flat-bottomed glass dish. Scatter the raspberries over the jelly roll. Make up the gelatin according to the directions on the package and pour it over the cake and fruit. Chill until set. Spoon the custard evenly over the gelatin, top with the cream or cream-and-yogurt mixture, and decorate with the chocolate.

Blueberry, Strawberry & Hazelnut Crisp

Everyone loves crisps, and toddlers are no exception. This version is particularly irresistible and, because of the nuts, highly nutritious.

MAKES 6 ADULT PORTIONS

1 *pint strawberries, rinsed and hulled*
1 *pint blueberries, rinsed*
2 *tablespoons sugar*
½ *cup turbinado sugar*

1 *cup toasted hazelnuts, finely chopped, or ground*
⅔ *cup whole-wheat flour*
1 *stick butter*

lace the fruit in a shallow baking dish and sprinkle the white sugar over it. Stir the turbinado sugar and hazelnuts into the flour and cut in the butter. Spoon the topping over the fruit, and smooth. Bake in an oven preheated to 400°F for 30–40 minutes. Serve with yogurt or cream.

Bread Pudding

Another classic that children love for its custard-like softness. The apricot jam makes this a little sweeter than usual; another selling point with under-fives.

MAKES 6 ADULT PORTIONS

½ cup golden raisins
2 tablespoons orange juice
1¼ cups milk
¼ cup sugar
1 vanilla bean

3 free-range eggs
⅔ cup heavy cream
8 thin slices of white bread, buttered
¼ cup apricot jam

Place the raisins and orange juice in a small bowl and soak for a few hours. Heat the milk with the sugar and vanilla bean, then let cool before removing the vanilla bean.

Beat together the eggs and cream, then stir the cooled milk into the eggs. Spread half the bread with the jam and sandwich together with the remaining slices. Cut off the crusts. Arrange the sandwiches in a shallow baking dish, then sprinkle the soaked raisins over them. Pour the milk and cream mixture over the sandwiches and let stand for about 1 hour. Place the dish in a deep roasting pan half-filled with hot water, and bake in an oven preheated to 325°F for 1 hour or until the top is crisp and golden. Serve warm rather than hot.

Spicy Apple Squares

A delicious snacktime treat, these moist fruity cakes are equally good served warm as a dessert, with custard.

MAKES 20

1½ cups peeled, cored, and chopped apples
½ cup sugar
½ cup brown sugar
¾ cup mixed nuts, finely chopped, or ground
1 teaspoon ground cinnamon

1 stick plus 1 tablespoon butter
2 free-range eggs
1½ cups self-rising flour, sifted
1 cup sour cream

Place the apples in a pan with 2 tablespoons of the white sugar, and cook gently until soft, then beat to make a coarse purée. Cream together the brown sugar, nuts, cinnamon, and 3 tablespoons of the butter.

Cream together the remaining butter and sugar, beat in the eggs and then fold in the sifted flour. Stir the sour cream into the batter. Grease and line an 8-inch square cake tin. Spoon in half the cake batter and smooth the top. Sprinkle with half the nut mixture, then spread the apple purée on the nuts. Cover with the remaining cake mixture and top with the remaining nut mixture. Bake in an oven preheated to 350°F for 1 hour, or until firm to the touch. Cool on a wire rack.

FESTIVE FOODS

Tomato & Cheese Straws

These look pretty, taste good, and can be dipped into anything from guacamole to yogurt and chive dip. Be warned, however: they are rather crumbly, so take measures to protect your prized Persian carpet! Frozen puff pastry is available at all major supermarkets.

MAKES 40

3 tablespoons sun-dried tomato paste
12 oz frozen puff pastry dough
black pepper to taste

2 teaspoons paprika
beaten free-range egg, to glaze
2 oz pecorino cheese, grated (½ cup)

Spread the sun-dried tomato paste over the dough, season with a little pepper and sprinkle with the paprika. Fold the pastry in half, brush with beaten egg and sprinkle with pecorino. Fold in half again, then roll out to the original size. Cut into 20 long, thin strips, then twist each strip several times and cut in half. Bake on a dampened baking sheet in an oven preheated to 425°F for 20 minutes. Cool on a wire rack.

Party Pizzas

Even very young children enjoy participating in creating their own party food. Prepare the crusts and spread with tomato sauce, then let your small guests choose their own toppings. For added infant appeal, make faces or spell their names with pieces of vegetable and grated cheese.

MAKES 8 x 8-inch PIZZAS

DOUGH
6 cups bread flour
2 teaspoons salt
2 teaspoons quick-rise active dry yeast
2½ cups lukewarm water mixed
with ¼ cup olive oil
TOMATO SAUCE
6 x 14-oz cans crushed tomatoes
3 tablespoons tomato paste

pinch of sugar
salt and black pepper to taste
TOPPINGS
mozzarella cheese, grated
fresh tomatoes, sliced
red peppers, roasted and sliced
baby corn, steamed
zucchini slices, roasted
mushrooms, sautéed

Sift the flour and salt together and stir in the yeast. Make a well in the middle of the flour, pour the water and olive oil into the well and mix to form a dough. Turn onto a lightly floured board and knead for 10 minutes or until smooth and elastic. Roll out and shape the dough into eight pizza crusts. Place on baking sheets, cover with oiled plastic film, and let rise in a warm place for 30 minutes.

While the dough is rising, place the tomato-sauce ingredients in a large pan, bring to a boil, and simmer for 20–30 minutes, until the sauce is thick and reduced. When the sauce is cool, spread a thin layer over each pizza crust. Arrange the different toppings in bowls. Allow your diminutive guests to choose their own topping preferences, then bake the pizzas in an oven preheated to 425°F for approximately 20 minutes.

Chestnut Rolls

My son adores these with a dish of sweet mango chutney as a dip. For older children, substitute chili powder for the paprika.

MAKES 48 ROLLS

8-oz can chestnuts in brine, puréed with a
little of the liquid
1 small onion, grated
1 small apple, peeled, cored, and grated
1 clove garlic, peeled and crushed

1 tablespoon lemon juice
1 tablespoon soy sauce
2 cups fresh white bread crumbs
pinch of paprika
8 oz frozen puff pastry dough, defrosted

Combine the chestnut purée, onion, apple, garlic, lemon juice, soy sauce, bread crumbs, and paprika, and let stand for 30 minutes. Cut the dough into strips approximately 1 inch wide. Roll the chestnut mixture into long, thin link-sausage shapes to fit the strips of dough. Dampen the dough edges, and roll the dough strips around the chestnut mixture. Prick the dough with a fork and cut into 1-inch pieces. Place the rolls seam-side down on a dampened baking sheet and bake in an oven preheated to 375°F for 10 minutes, or until crisp and golden.

Mini Cheese Sausages

Serve these tasty mini sausages cold on toothpicks with an Apple Purée dip (see page 23), and watch them disappear.

MAKES 16

3 cups fresh whole-wheat bread crumbs
4 oz sharp cheddar cheese, grated (1 cup)
1 onion, peeled and grated
1 tablespoon finely chopped fresh flat-leaf parsley

½ teaspoon dry mustard
salt and black pepper to taste
1 free-range egg, beaten with a little milk
flour for coating
vegetable oil for cooking

Mix together the bread crumbs, cheese, onion, parsley, mustard, and seasonings. Bind the mixture with egg and a little milk (the amount depends on how dry the bread crumbs are). Divide the mixture into sixteen pieces, and shape into small link sausages. Roll the sausages in flour, then chill for at least 30 minutes. Pan-fry in a little vegetable oil until golden brown all over, about 5 minutes.

Potato Dippers

These are also known to my son as big fries, which for him makes them a better medium for his beloved tomato sauce. Children with less predictable palates may be persuaded to appreciate them with a sour cream-and-chive dip. For children, like mine, who love garlic, crush a clove into the oil before brushing it on the potato wedges.

MAKES 20

5 medium-sized baking potatoes
6 tablespoons olive oil
salt

Scrub the potatoes and cut each into four wedges. Boil them rapidly for 5 minutes, then drain, and return them to the pan. Cover and shake vigorously (this roughens up the surfaces for a crunchy result). Heat the oil in a roasting pan, add the potatoes, and turn them to coat with the oil. Sprinkle with salt and bake in an oven preheated to 425°F for 30–40 minutes or until golden and crunchy.

Mini Veggie Burgers

Parents of vegetarian children can avoid the burger issue as much as they like, but sooner or later all toddlers will become aware of an institution called McDonald's, and want to know why they don't eat burgers. The answer to this, of course, is that they do—and better ones at that.

MAKES 8–10

1 tablespoon olive oil
1 small onion, peeled and grated
1 small red pepper, seeded and finely chopped
2 cloves garlic, peeled and finely chopped
1½ lb reconstituted TVP mince—follow

directions on package
1 free-range egg, beaten
salt and black pepper to taste
flour for coating
vegetable oil for cooking burgers

Heat the olive oil, add the onion and pepper, and cook until the vegetables are soft and just beginning to brown. Add the garlic, cook for another minute, then transfer the mixture to a bowl. Add the TVP mince, beaten egg, and seasonings. Mix thoroughly. Shape into eight small burgers, lightly coat in flour and pan-fry in hot oil until brown on both sides. Serve in mini rolls with lettuce and ketchup.

Frozen Fruity Yogurt

"I scream, you scream, everybody screams for ice cream …" This scrumptious, healthy alternative puts most commercial creations to shame. Mango, strawberry, and pineapple are good choices for the fruit purée. (Just pop the flesh into a food processor with a little sugar, if required, and whiz to a smooth pulp.)

MAKES 4–6 PORTIONS

1¼ cups fruit purée
⅔ cups each plain yogurt and heavy cream, mixed

Whiz the fruit and yogurt together in a food processor to combine thoroughly. Transfer to a shallow freezerproof container and freeze for 1–2 hours. When ice crystals begin to form around the edge of the container, return the mixture to the food processor and blend until smooth. Return the mixture to the freezer and freeze until solid. Let stand at room temperature for 15 minutes before serving.

Animal Crackers

Most children find anthropomorphic eats enjoyable, so use animal-shaped cutters to turn these cookies into barnyard friends.

MAKES 10–16

1 stick butter, softened
3 tablespoons superfine sugar
finely grated peel of ½ orange

⅔ cup all-purpose flour
3 tablespoons cornstarch
1½ oz flaked coconut

Cream together the butter, sugar, and orange peel. Add the remaining ingredients and beat to form a dough ball. Roll out the dough on a lightly floured board and cut out shapes using animal cutters. Place the cookies on non-oiled baking sheets and bake in an oven preheated to 325°F for 15 minutes. Cool on a wire rack.

☺ ☹

Party People

Use dried currants, candied cherries, and chocolate chips to lend character
to these face-shaped cookies.

MAKES 40 COOKIES

3 cups all-purpose flour
1 teaspoon baking powder
¼ teaspoon salt
2 sticks butter
1 cup superfine sugar
2 free-range eggs
few drops vanilla extract

FROSTING
1½ cups confectioners' sugar, sifted
1 tablespoon butter, softened
4 teaspoons boiling water
chocolate chips, candied cherries,
dried currants, and tiny chocolate
strands to decorate

Sift together the flour, baking powder, and salt. Cut in the butter. Stir in the superfine sugar. Beat the eggs with the vanilla extract and stir into the flour mixture to form a dough. Roll out the dough thinly on a lightly floured board, cut out rounds using a 3-inch cutter and place on oiled baking sheets. Bake in an oven preheated to 350°F for 12 minutes until golden and beginning to brown at the edges. Cool on a wire rack. Mix together the frosting ingredients and coat each cookie smoothly. Decorate with chocolate chips for eyes, slivers of candied cherry for lips, currants for noses, and chocolate strands for hair.

Chocolate Raisin Bars

Ridiculously rich, and irresistibly chocolatey, this party treat never fails to please both children and adults.

MAKES 16 PIECES

8 oz graham crackers, crushed
1 cup raisins
1 stick butter
1 tablespoon brown sugar

3 tablespoons unsweetened cocoa powder
4 tablespoons golden syrup, such as Lyle's
8 oz semisweet chocolate

Place the crushed crackers and raisins in a large bowl. Melt the butter, sugar, cocoa powder, and syrup together over low heat. Combine the butter mixture with the cracker crumbs and raisins. Press the mixture into an oiled 8-inch square pan and leave to cool. Melt the chocolate in a bowl over simmering water until smooth, then spread it over the top of the cooled cracker mixture. Mark into squares and leave to cool thoroughly before cutting.

TODDLER MENU CHART

Now that your toddler is able to join in family meals, try to tailor his or her diet to fit in with yours. This suggested Menu Chart should help you plan accordingly.

INGREDIENTS CHECKLIST

Apricot spread
Baked beans
Breads and muffins
Breakfast cereals
Cheese
Chocolate
Coconut milk
Corn, canned
Cream
Chips
Dried fruit
Eggs
Fresh fruit and
  vegetables
Frozen vegetables
Fruit juices
Graham crackers
Haricot beans, canned
Herbs and spices
Honey
Lasagne
Lentils, canned
Marmite/Vegemite
Mixed nuts
Molasses
Oatmeal
Olives, ripe
Pasta shapes and rice
Peanut butter
Raspberry gelatin
  crystals
Raspberry jelly roll
Red kidney beans,
  canned
Sesame oil
Soy sauce
Sugar
Sun-dried tomato
  paste
Tofu
Tomatoes, canned
Tomato paste
TVP (textured
  vegetable protein)
Vegetarian hot dogs
  and sausages
Yogurt, plain

	Breakfast	Lunch	Afternoon snack	Dinner	Bedtime
Day 1	Weetabix and banana	Stir-fried Vegetables with rice Bread Pudding	Cream Cheese & Bean Slices Fruit	Carrot & Orange Soup Garlic Bread Yogurt	Milk
Day 2	Scrambled egg on toast Orange segments	Vegetarian Sausage & Apple Casserole Frozen Fruity Yogurt	Tomato & Cheese Straws Apple	Pasta with Beefless Spaghetti Sauce Fruit	Milk
Day 3	Oatmeal with dried apricots Marmite toast	Cauliflower & Potato Bake Peas Blueberry, Strawberry & Hazelnut Crisp	Peanut Butter & Banana Fingers Plain yogurt with fruit purée	Wild West Beans Vegetarian hot dogs Fruit	Milk
Day 4	Muffin Rabbits Peach or pear	Vegetable Curry with banana, yogurt and rice Fruit	Italian Flag Rolls Spicy Apple Squares	Potato Dippers Salad Plain yogurt with fruit purée	Milk
Day 5	Grilled cheese and tomato sandwich Fruit	Spinach & Mushroom Lasagne Salad Yogurt	Potato Cakes Apple Purée Raspberry Trifle	Frittata Baked beans Fruit	Milk
Day 6	Cornflakes Strawberries Cinnamon toast	Paella Thomas' Lemon Tart	Mini Veggie Burgers Fruit	Leek Tart Tomato salad Plain yogurt with fruit purée	Milk
Day 7	Boiled egg with Marmite toast strips Grapes	Bread & Cheese Pudding Grated apple and carrot salad Yogurt	Baked Potato with Ratatouille Chocolate Baked Bananas	Four Seasons Soup Cheese & Herb Scones Fruit	Milk

INDEX

EDDISON•SADD EDITIONS

Editor.................Vivienne Wells
Proof Reader.........Nikky Twyman
Indexer..............Dorothy Frame
Art Director.....Elaine Partington
Art Editor..............Pritty Ramjee
Illustrator.............Stephen May
Production...........Hazel Kirkman and Katrina Macnab